INSANITY DEFENSE

INSANITY DEFENSE

WHY OUR FAILURE

TO CONFRONT

HARD PROBLEMS

MAKES US LESS SAFE

CONGRESSWOMAN

JANE HARMAN

St. Martin's Press
New York

Library of Congress Cataloging-in-Publication Data

Names: Harman, Jane, author.
Title: Insanity defense : why our failure to confront hard
    national security problems makes us less safe / Jane Harman.
Description: First edition. | New York : St. Martin's Press,
    2021. | Includes bibliographical references and index.
Identifiers: LCCN 2020053517 | ISBN 9781250758774
    (hardcover) | ISBN 9781250758781 (ebook)
Subjects: LCSH: National security—United States. |
    Intelligence service—United States. | United States—
    Military policy. | United States—Foreign relations—1989–
Classification: LCC UA23 .H36414 2021 | DDC
    355/.033073—dc23
LC record available at https://lccn.loc.gov/2020053517

To my perfect grandchildren:
Lucy, Will, Henry, Matt,
Charlie, Sadie, Nora, and Lila

CONTENTS

INSANITY DEFENSE

INTRODUCTION

Insanity Defense

"The House believes the war on terror has been its own worst enemy." I was asked to argue this proposition before the Oxford Union for a debate on October 28, 2018. At first I was uncomfortable accepting the invitation. The topic was provocative. The setting—the world's oldest and most prestigious debating society—was intimidating. But I screwed up my courage and joined the team arguing for the proposition. As I worked through my presentation and supporting arguments, I realized how central the issue is to explaining America's mistakes in national security policy. The culprits are hubris, complacency, and an inability to comprehend a world in which others may reject our political values and economic model.

Everyone knows that the definition of insanity is doing the same thing over and over and expecting a different result. My work in the defense and intelligence space spans more than three decades, and I am vexed by the fact that policies designed to protect America are actually making us *less* safe. I call this "insanity defense": doing the same thing again and again and expecting it to enhance our security. This book chronicles how four administrations have failed to confront some of the toughest policy issues, and it suggests achievable policy fixes that can move us toward a safer future. It is also an account by someone who was, to paraphrase the score from the musical *Hamilton*, in the rooms where it happened.

Consider the track record of the past thirty years:

- Slashing defense and intelligence spending at the end of the Cold War without a strategy for what the world would look like, then defaulting to military force repeatedly after 9/11 with increasingly dismal results.

- Blowing off multiple terrorism warnings and then creating a homeland security apparatus neglected and misused by successive presidents and Congresses. If 9/11 was a wake-up call, then COVID-19 is a five-alarm fire for revamping how we prepare and respond to security threats.

- Running the intelligence community on a 1947 business model, reforming it after the Iraq debacle, then undermining it through repeated purges of experienced career leadership.

- Ignoring the Constitution and the Geneva Conventions when detaining and interrogating so-called enemy combatants in the name of preventing the next attack; when faced with the ugly consequences, failing to enact a sustainable legal framework.

- Failing to use the lawful tools available to prevent post-9/11 terror attacks, then adopting a massive extrajudicial domestic surveillance program; now letting recently adopted legal provisions lapse, potentially leaving America dangerously exposed.

- Allowing successive presidents to ignore constitutional checks and balances, most egregiously after 9/11, with military operations, drone strikes, and arms sales launched without congressional approval or oversight.

- The Congress, weakened by toxic partisanship, enabling its own demise as a coequal branch of government by failing to replace the 2001 Authorization for the Use of Military Force (AUMF) and conceding other powers to the executive, all at a time when bipartisan consensus and action are needed to take on America's hardest problems.

For most of this period I was there: as witness, legislator, exhorter, enabler, dissident, and, eventually, outside advisor and commentator. Before 9/11, I confronted the impact of defense and intelligence cuts on my aerospace-dependent congressional district—and, ultimately, on America's national security capabilities—in an era when domestic concerns dominated the political agenda. After 9/11, I was a leading congressional voice on intelligence and counterterrorism issues. I had the opportunity to play a role in the Bush administration's efforts to fashion a new security architecture in the years following the attacks. When bipartisan cooperation was still valued, President George W. Bush made a point of cultivating a group of us on the Democratic side. I was invited to high-level meetings and, as the ranking member of the House intelligence committee (that is, the most senior Democrat on the committee, which at the time was controlled by Republicans), received the most-classified briefings. I crafted key legislation with Republican counterparts, creating new government structures for homeland security and national intelligence. I also provided bipartisan support for some policies and approaches—on detentions, surveillance, and military intervention—that I later came to regret.

After leaving the Congress, I continued to engage on these issues from my perch as president and CEO of the nonpartisan Woodrow Wilson International Center for Scholars. There I succeeded my friend and mentor Congressman Lee Hamilton, who co-chaired the 9/11 Commission from what later became my office. As an observer, analyst, and in some cases advisor, I saw the Obama administration attempt to "turn the page" on the war on terror while continuing with many of the same approaches—if not policies and people—as the Bush-Cheney administration: an escalating drone assassination campaign, a military "surge" in Afghanistan, and a policymaking approach that, in conjunction with a swollen White House staff, marginalized the administration's own cabinet departments along with the Congress. And despite the rhetoric about ending "endless wars," the Trump administration followed roughly the same playbook as its predecessors: more drone strikes and Special Forces raids, continued use of the detention camp at Guantanamo Bay Naval Base, and more troop deployments and arms sales to support autocrats in the Middle East.

The political and strategic entropy is real and cannot be ignored. The reasons are varied and complex, in some cases going back generations. American leaders didn't realize soon enough that the institutions and habits formed during the Cold War were no longer effective in an increasingly multi-power world transformed by digital technology and riven by ethno-sectarian conflict. Nations that became rising centers of economic and political power, freed from the fear of the Soviets, no longer deferred to America as before. Yet we settled into a comfortable, at times arrogant, position as the lone superpower or "indispensable nation." At the same time our governing institutions, which had stayed resilient, however imperfectly, through multiple crises, began their own unraveling. Our post–Cold War miscalculations and vulnerabilities were exposed traumatically on September 11, 2001, and have not been fundamentally addressed in the years since.

To be sure, I have some great stories to tell. But this is not a typical political memoir or retrospective. Arguably, the time for that book was soon after I left the Congress in 2011, when memories were clearer, passions were hotter, and leading personalities (and culprits) were still in office. This is a story of people—leaders who strove to do their best under complex circumstances but were too often undermined by personal, ideological, or bureaucratic blind spots. In many respects, it is also a story of institutions: their cultures, their processes, and, too often, their inability to adapt from an industrial-age analog mindset to our digital world.

The U.S. intelligence community (IC) was the focus for most of my time in the Congress.[1] I have great affection and respect for those toiling in the shadows to protect our country, often at great personal risk. I pushed to ensure they had sufficient funding, tools, and authority to do their jobs, and pushed back when they were scapegoated unfairly, including after 9/11. But I also became disillusioned as legitimate requests by the Congress were ignored and trust was shattered. Until recently it was the political left that tended to be most skeptical of America's intelligence agencies, due to Cold War–era abuses. A large segment on the right still believes a "deep state" conspired against President Trump. Our IC is the so-called tip of the spear in confronting threats against us, everything from terrorism to great power competition to global pandemics. We undermine the IC at great risk to America.

By necessity, presidential power will always grow during times of conflict and crisis. Temporarily shrunk by the end of the Cold War and the distractions created by partisan investigations and impeachment, the White House would rebound

---

1 The IC consists of the Central Intelligence Agency (CIA); eight elements from the Department of Defense focused on collection and analysis of electronic, satellite, and military information; and the intelligence divisions of seven other cabinet departments and agencies (all coordinated by the Office of the Director of National Intelligence, created in 2004).

with a vengeance after 9/11. I watched up close as multiple administrations operated with an expansive view of the president's authority as commander in chief. The most egregious executive branch abuses of the Bush-Cheney era were pared back by Congress over time. But a new administration promising "hope and change" would cling just as tenaciously to executive prerogatives with respect to warmaking, counterterrorism, and secrecy.

I spent seventeen years in the Congress as an elected representative and, much earlier in my career, five years as a lawyer and committee staff in the Senate. My time on Capitol Hill is the source of some of my dearest and most enduring friendships with members of both political parties.

Article I of the Constitution provides Congress significant authority and responsibilities in national security, too often unexercised. Notwithstanding some genuine bipartisan achievements before and after 9/11, Congress's role in national security has succumbed to the toxic and divisive forces that began to permeate electoral politics in the 1980s and 1990s. Years later we still lack a coherent and politically sustainable comprehensive legal framework for dealing with surveillance, detention, and interrogation of terror suspects. Guantanamo is still in business, and the main perpetrators of 9/11 remain there in tropical captivity, untried and unconvicted.

This book is an explanation, from one participant's informed—but hardly omniscient—perspective, of how we got here: the series of fits and starts, insights, and misjudgments that

put the United States in the position it is in today. America
cannot afford a fourth lost decade while threats continue to
rise. Yet, as a government and as a nation, we seem to cycle over and over through the same problems and make the
same mistakes again and again; this is the definition of insanity. The chapters in this book discuss seven national security challenges that have been addressed inadequately or, in
some cases, barely addressed at all. In addition to critiquing
the failures and omissions that brought us to this point, this
book suggests politically realistic pathways to make significant progress on, if not solve, these perennial hard problems.

ONE

Paying the Price for
Over-Militarizing Security

I walked into Rayburn 2118, the stately hearing room for the House Armed Services Committee. It was February 24, 1993, and I had been in office just a few weeks. As the most junior committee member, I took the last seat on the lower dais, eye level with the top Pentagon brass testifying on the defense budget. The committee's chair, Ron Dellums, a marine and community activist turned congressman from Berkeley, California, opened the hearing: "For the first time in forty-five years we are in a 'window of opportunity' where we do not face a major military threat from abroad." In the coming months Dellums posed a series of fundamental questions about America's national security policies and institutions. Were the threats more economic and technological than military? Dellums pointed out that the United States did not have a road map for this post–Cold War world. Indeed, we had no real strategy. We were just "treading water." Few good answers were forthcoming from either the generals or the members of the committee, including me.

We didn't realize it at the time, but the lack of such a strategic road map would have disastrous consequences. Massive

cuts to the defense and intelligence procurement budgets by
the administration of President George H. W. Bush (often referred to as "Bush 41" to distinguish his administration from
that of his son George W. Bush, or "Bush 43") hollowed out
America's aerospace industry and skilled workforce, which are
so necessary to maintain military superiority. They also crushed
my aerospace-dependent congressional district. A diminished
military would not, however, stop the United States from
pursuing a series of foreign deployments during the 1990s against
countries that posed no serious security threat to America.
Over that same period the growing terror threat got inadequate
attention. After 9/11, we declared a "war on terror" that
resulted in a series of military interventions, none more disastrous than Iraq. The result has been more instability, more
terrorists, and calls for yet larger military budgets. At the same
time, tools of "soft power" that could bring more of the world
to our side were underfunded and undermined.

A saner approach then—and now—would be to live our
values as Americans and defeat bad ideas (terrorism and au-
thoritarianism) with good ideas (freedom and human dignity).
That would require a significant investment in diplomacy,
development, and other means of persuasion and inspiration.
America will always need a strong military and a willingness to
use it, but we can be much smarter about how much we spend
on defense—and where.

The roots of America's post-9/11 national security fumbles
go back to our response to the end of the Cold War. In many

respects the 1990s represented a lost decade. I had a front-row seat and was often in the room as a member of the congressional class of 1992, the first elected after the final collapse of the Soviet Union. When I took office in January 1993 the "peace dividend" declared by the Bush 41 administration was widely touted.

What was a dividend for most of the country turned out to be an economic disaster for my congressional district, which ran along the Pacific coast of Los Angeles County and included many small cities that were home to most of California's satellite production. We did not have big assembly plants churning out hundreds of vehicles and aircraft. What the South Bay, as the area is known, did produce was some of the most technically sophisticated and sensitive assets of the U.S. intelligence enterprise. More important was the human capital—not so many wrench turners, but quite a few of what I called the "triple PhDs who won the Cold War." As I told the *Los Angeles Times* during my 1992 campaign: "This is a community of people terrified about losing jobs who have enormously sophisticated training and skills."

I had asked to join the House Permanent Select Committee on Intelligence (HPSCI)—a so-called leadership committee, with plum appointments made by the Speaker of the House. I already had a close relationship with Speaker Tom Foley. But he told me he had to give the last remaining seat on HPSCI to a fellow Californian who was senior to me: Nancy Pelosi.

Instead I joined the House Armed Services Committee (HASC)—my second choice, but still important to my

district. It was during one such HASC hearing that Ron
Dellums posed serious questions about America's strategic
priorities after the Cold War. The questions he posed were
the right ones, both back then and, in many respects, still
today.

Strategy is not just a set of goals and aspirations. A real
strategy sets priorities and makes trade-offs. What is *not*
done is often more important than what is done. During the
Cold War our strategy was to defeat communism, a battle
that basically split the world into two teams. After the fall of
the Soviet Union, a handful of senior officials in the Bush
41 Pentagon, supported by a number of conservative writers
and analysts, suggested a rather extreme strategy: seize the
historical opportunity to establish untrammeled U.S. hege-
mony, a global Pax Americana sustained by a military as
large and powerful as it had been during the Cold War, if
not more so.

But few people in either political party were inclined to
go in that direction. Or really any direction, as U.S. foreign policy became increasingly ad hoc and personality-
driven. Some in the Congress close to President Clinton
pressed hard to intervene in Haiti—so he did. NATO
was expanded to encompass many of the former Warsaw
Pact nations, right up to the borders of the former Soviet Union. Knowledgeable people have different views
on the wisdom of moving NATO eastward. As the original author of the policy of containment, George Kennan,
pointed out, this move would certainly exacerbate Russian
fears and insecurities. But UN ambassador Madeleine Al-

bright, with her inspiring personal story as a refugee from behind the Iron Curtain, carried the day within the Clinton administration.

Some of us hoped the Cold War could give way to a more noble purpose. Military force could be used for the sake of good in places where ethnic cleansing and other human rights abuses violated core moral values. A talented young war correspondent named Samantha Power came up with the foreign policy principle of "responsibility to protect." But as a practical matter, European allies had to be on board with any proposed military action, and the risk of casualties had to be close to zero. The Balkans would become the scene of U.S.-led military interventions—albeit limited to airpower and conducted well after the worst atrocities were committed. The genocide in Rwanda was left to burn itself out, much to the later anguish of a young State Department official named Susan Rice. At the time I largely supported Clinton's foreign policy—from NATO expansion to the Kosovo air campaign—though with lingering reservations.

In the absence of real strategy and with defense budgets shrinking, congressional and Pentagon leaders chose to focus on raw numbers: personnel, weapons platforms, and pork. The assumption was that future conflicts would resemble a scaled-down version of the Gulf War (which ended in 1991) or possibly the Korean War (which ended in 1953), with lots of tanks, fighters, and warships doing a better job of what they'd done for decades—fighting other large armies, navies, and air forces. General Colin Powell, near the end of his tenure as chair of the Joint Chiefs of Staff, had endorsed the concept of a "base force" large enough to fight two regional wars at the same time.

Yet it should have been evident even then that the threats to America, indeed the character of conflict, were fundamentally changing. Just one month into my first term, in late February 1993, Middle Eastern terrorists attempted to take down New York's World Trade Center with a vehicle bomb. Shortly thereafter the U.S. public watched in horror as the bodies of American helicopter pilots were dragged through the streets of Mogadishu by Somali militants. International forces were ambushed there using tactics similar to what soldiers and marines would face a decade later in Iraq. Flush with Cold War victory, we failed to appreciate the significance of these events and chose to focus on other, mostly domestic, concerns. The World Trade Center perpetrators were arrested and ultimately convicted, given long prison sentences. The main lesson from Somalia? No more U.S. boots on the ground, at least in Africa.

In the summer of 1993, Congress dived into debating and approving a defense budget that in constant dollars was about a third less than it had been at the height of the Reagan defense buildup. The chief executives of America's aerospace and defense firms were summoned to the Pentagon for what was called "the Last Supper," at which they were informed there would not be enough money to go around to support so many companies—they would have to merge to survive. From about a dozen so-called prime contractors we ended up with six by the end of the decade.[2] Such consolidation was necessary, perhaps, but it translated into less competition and innovation.

Under those circumstances, congressional oversight by the House Armed Services Committee devolved into what I called a "widget protection" program. I don't intend to come across as sanctimonious; I could fairly be labeled a "widget protector" at the time. For example, in 1993 I pulled out all the stops to prevent the Los Angeles Air Force Base from being moved to Colorado, and in 1995 I fought to prevent it from being closed. I advocated for Southern California programs outside my district as well—C-17 cargo planes in Long Beach, the B-2 bomber in Palmdale. (One of my vivid—and somewhat embarrassing—early memories was of trying to climb onto the massive B-2 in a skirt and heels.) Two area firms, Hughes Aerospace and McDonnell Douglas (which built the C-17), were later acquired by Boeing; after practicing some "tough love" toward Boeing when a satellite procurement went off the tracks, I would become known as "Boeing's mother."

But good local politics can also produce good national defense. While most of the U.S. military's major platforms had been recapitalized (that is, replaced with newer, more advanced submarines, combat vehicles, ships, missiles, and aircraft) during the Reagan administration, much of the

---

2 Lockheed Martin, Boeing, Raytheon, Northrop Grumman, General Dynamics, and the U.S. subsidiary of British Aerospace (BAE).

air force's mobility fleet—refueling tankers and cargo—was going on thirty years of service life at the time (and today some tankers are older still, put into service more than a half century ago). And no matter what the future held, America would always need top-flight surveillance and reconnaissance satellites—the kind made in my district. If anything, in a fragmenting world—nations splitting into multiple states, radical movements arising from the ashes—we would need more situational awareness capacity, not less.

Unfortunately, the 1990s saw the United States go in the opposite direction with respect to space capabilities. My district paid the social and economic price then, and our country is paying a strategic price today. Early in the 1990s, the top employer in the South Bay was Hughes Aerospace, with more than 5,000 employees working in El Segundo. In 1988, defense-related projects accounted for 85 percent of Hughes's revenue. When I accompanied deputy defense secretary William Perry in June 1993 for a tour of Hughes, that proportion had fallen to about 50 percent.

The following year (February 1994) I testified as a witness—unusual for a junior representative—before the House Intelligence Committee. I pointed out that "if action is not taken now to stabilize the intelligence industrial base, we could lose important capabilities that have required years to develop . . . losses likely to be permanent, because the companies and the workforce that make up this industrial base will not be around when the Federal government decides in three or six or ten years that it needs them again." Once these workers retired or gave up in frustration, their critically important skill set would go with them—human capital that would take years, perhaps even decades, to reconstitute.

I urged the committee to "consider letting intelligence suppliers commercialize their capabilities, where doing so does not undermine U.S. security." One example entailed using a common satellite "bus," or basic model, for both defense and commercial purposes. Then there were exports of U.S. commercial satellites to help keep American aerospace providers healthy. A political scandal later in the decade involving the satellite communications company Loral and information that was revealed in violation of the Arms Export Control Act would prompt Congress to make it extremely difficult for U.S. firms to sell overseas—for export control purposes, commercial satellites were now treated like cruise missiles. According to the Aerospace Industries Association, the U.S. global market share of satellite exports fell from 75 percent in 1995 to 25 percent in 2005.

During my third term, from 1997 to 1999, I finally got the coveted seat on HPSCI. It was an entry into a world that, intellectually, represented the high point of my Hill experience. The United States no longer had to worry about the Soviet Union, but a toxic admixture of other perils had emerged out of its ashes and from the shadows in other parts of the globe. These included Al Qaeda, a transnational terrorist network headed by the charismatic son of a Saudi construction magnate—a group that had taken credit for destroying two U.S. embassies in East Africa the previous August. The growing ideological and security threats from Islamic extremism, which should have been apparent since 1993, were finally getting the attention they were due—at least by HPSCI. The CIA was well into the fight against Al Qaeda—or at least trying to be. But it was apparent even then that the U.S. government overall, including the Congress, was not well organized or, frankly, motivated to deal with a threat unlike any we'd faced before.

The phone call came sometime in early June 1999. The House minority leader, Richard Gephardt, was on the line. The prior summer I had come up short in the Democratic primary for governor of California, a quest that required me to give up my House seat. In recent months there had been rumblings in California political circles that I might have another go at the seat I had relinquished for the governor's race, though an April 7 Associated Press headline had mostly quashed them: "Former Congresswoman Will Not Seek Her Old Seat." I initially assumed Gephardt, with hopes of taking back Democratic control of the House in 2000, was trying to change my mind (again) about running. But after some brief pleasantries he got right to the point: would I be willing to serve as a member of the newly authorized National Commission on Terrorism? I didn't think twice, accepting immediately—and eagerly.

In Washington, D.C., appointing outside commissions to "study" a problem is often seen as a way to avoid dealing with the problem, especially one that is complex and controversial. I did not see this terrorism commission in that light at all; if I had, I would not have joined. Rather, it was a congressionally chartered response to the 1998 Al Qaeda bombings of U.S. embassies in East Africa. Before leaving Congress, I had seen the intelligence showing Al Qaeda growing in power, reach, and ambition. It also helped that the commission was chaired by a former senior State Department official, L. Paul "Jerry" Bremer, a protégé of Henry Kissinger who had served as ambassador to the Netherlands. A Yale and Harvard graduate, son of the former president of Christian Dior Perfumes, he was known at the time as one of the country's most talented diplomats. He'd also been a counterterrorism chief at the State Department.

My prior committee assignments on defense and intelligence had schooled me to some degree on the issues involved. But this commission was the deepest dive by any American nongovernmental body into the global terrorism problem since the end of the Cold War. There were other outside commissions doing excellent work relating to terrorism, most notably the panel led by former senators Gary Hart and Warren Rudman. But ours was singularly focused on global terrorism in all its dimensions—ideological, diplomatic, financial—and the readiness of the U.S. government to prevent or respond to a major attack. The commission was a diverse, bipartisan group. (I was the only member who had run for political office.) We got the necessary security clearances, traveled the world, and met with people inside and outside government—U.S. and allied intelligence agencies, academics, NGOs, and more.

While I was working on the commission, the "seduction of Jane" campaign (as I called it) by Gephardt and other Democratic congressional leaders continued, and eventually it achieved its intended result: in December I declared officially my intention to run for my former congressional seat. The early stages of the campaign still left plenty of time to focus on the commission, which wrapped up its work and published the report "Countering the Changing Threat of International Terrorism" in June 2000.

Our report, in retrospect, demonstrated the limitations of even the most expert and sophisticated assumptions about terrorism. We correctly identified the emergence of a new brand of terrorists, who are "less dependent on state sponsorship and are, instead, forming loose, transnational affiliations based on religious or ideological affinity and a common hatred of the United States . . . [which] makes terrorist attacks more difficult to detect and prevent." Al Qaeda had effectively declared war on the United States with a 1996 "fatwa," and shortly after the East Africa bombings, CIA director George Tenet declared war on Al Qaeda in an internal message (though his posture did not extend to the rest of the IC, the Pentagon, the Congress, or the White House).

But the traditional paradigm of state sponsorship of terrorism still loomed large. Ideological groups active in Europe during the Cold War remained very much in memory. Readers of the report will be surprised by the number of mentions of Greece, where there had been 146 attacks against Americans since 1975, only one of which was solved (we recommended that Greece and Pakistan both be cited for "not cooperating fully" in counterterror efforts—prompting angry responses from both countries' embassies). The most recent horrific attack involving American civilians—besides Oklahoma City—was the 1988 downing of Pan Am flight 103 over Scotland at the direction of Libyan intelligence services. Before 9/11, the greatest killer of American troops and diplomats overseas was Hezbollah and related groups, supported by Iran. They were considered responsible for the bombings in 1983 of the U.S. embassy and Marine Corps barracks in Beirut—killing more than 250 American troops and diplomats—and the 1996 attack on Khobar Towers in Saudi Arabia, which killed nineteen U.S. Air Force personnel being housed there and wounded hundreds of other people. Hezbollah, still an Iranian proxy group, also bombed Jewish sites in Buenos Aires in 1995, which showed they had the reach to attack the Western Hemisphere.

Iran would be mentioned in the report more than any other terrorism source—thirty-three times (Al Qaeda was mentioned four times). Afghanistan received some attention as the known home of Al Qaeda leader Osama Bin Laden, but the report focused more on the official U.S. list of state sponsors of terrorism. The Taliban was not then recognized as a state. Iraq was not mentioned once.

Four months later, an Al Qaeda–linked suicide bomber on a speedboat struck the USS *Cole*, anchored in a Yemeni harbor, killing seventeen sailors and nearly sinking the ship. With the U.S. presidential election less than a month away, the response to the *Cole* bombing would be left to the next administration. The presidential candidates, Al Gore and

George W. Bush, issued statements of condemnation and resolve. Then, immediately after the election, nearly all media
and government attention turned to the Florida recount and
the issue of hanging chads.

In January 2001, the Hart–Rudman Commission issued
the third and final installment of its two-year study, "Roadmap for National Security, Imperative for Change." Com-
missioned originally by the Defense Department, this was
supposed to be a comprehensive assessment of all national security challenges. Yet, as Rudman testified after 9/11, the group
kept coming back to homeland security and terrorism—rather
than conventional military threats—as the overwhelming
priority. The report's first installment, in 1999, said: "Large
numbers of Americans will die on American soil, victims
of terrorism, in the coming century." Its final installment
shaved the time frame for these deaths to the next twenty-
five years.

September 11 was so catastrophic that referring to it as a
crime—which it was, albeit on a massive scale—seemed inadequate. For many people, the most devastating attack ever on
U.S. soil had to be an act of war, which called on us to wage
war in response. Thus the phrase "war on terror" was coined
almost immediately. Apart from being illogical—terror is a
tactic—the phrase played into the hands of Al Qaeda by el-
evating them from criminals to combatants (holy warriors
or mujahedin, as they saw it, and as they effectively sold it).
The phrase "war on terror" and more consequentially the

mentality that informed it, would prove costly—hundreds of thousands of lives, trillions of dollars, millions displaced, a region shattered, adherents of a major world religion alienated, and other consequences we still can't predict. It would also deplete the resources and leadership bandwidth needed to protect the homeland—or to pursue diplomatic and political avenues that leaders could use, by working closely with allies and new partners, to make America safer. Over the next decade the fear of another 9/11-style attack would ease. But the war on terror—military deployments and follow-on "surges," drone strikes, and other "kinetic" measures—would march on apace.

The Congress passed an Authorization to Use Military Force on September 13, 2001. It was worded broadly to give the president latitude. Nearly two decades later, as will be discussed later, that AUMF is still being used to authorize a variety of military operations. Afghanistan would turn out to be a long, frustrating, and ultimately unpopular campaign. But there we had little choice but to strike hard with military force—at least initially. The timid U.S. reactions to past terror attacks—Bin Laden had taken note of America's aversion to any military casualties during the 1990s—demanded a major correction.

To the extent America was going to have a "war on terror" in a militarized sense, Afghanistan is where it should have begun—and ended. But, of course, it would not end there. I believe, though it is hard to prove, that the relative ease of the initial Afghan campaign turned out to be a curse, as it led many Americans to believe that our military was invincible and history was on our side. This attitude led to the invasion of Iraq. A tough, prolonged fight to topple the Taliban in Afghanistan might have spared the United States—and the people of the Middle East—much agony later on.

Intelligence experts define "black swans" as shocking world-historical events: Pearl Harbor, the Yom Kippur War, the fall of the shah of Iran, the Soviet invasion of Afghanistan, and—the blackest of them all—the 9/11 attacks. For all the reforms to intelligence systems—and pledges of "never again"—these surprises are almost impossible to avoid. According to Israeli scholar Martin Kramer, the key is not "in predicting black swans, but in responding to them. Each . . . is an opportunity to be either seized or wasted." Kramer concludes that the Bush 43 team "wasted their black swan" following 9/11. With the rest of the world recoiling in horror at what Al Qaeda had done, and with sympathy and support for the United States at an all-time high (even in Iran), the opportunity existed to, in Kramer's words, "forge a new paradigm out of the wreckage." Instead of a new paradigm, we got Iraq, waterboarding, surges, and drones.

The proposition that Saddam Hussein was a serious threat was uncontroversial among national security officials and experts from both parties. The Clinton administration spent billions each year policing a no-fly zone over Iraq and launched a multiday bombing campaign in 1998 after UN weapons inspectors withdrew in frustration. Bush upped the ante by citing the "Axis of Evil" (Iraq, Iran, and North Korea) in his January 2002 State of the Union address. Then in September, one year after the 9/11 attacks, the administration issued a new National Security Strategy. Various strategy documents are required by Congress but usually make for soporific reading. Not this time. President Bush declared that the United States "must be prepared to stop rogue states and their terrorist clients before they are able to threaten or use weapons of mass destruction against the United States and our allies and friends." (Even after 9/11, the administration seemed more focused on state actors—countries with borders and governments—instead of the loosely organized transnational groups that had begun to emerge as major terrorism sponsors.) "To forestall or prevent such hostile acts by our adversaries," the strategy concluded, "the United States will, if necessary, act preemptively."

Hence the doctrine of preemption was unveiled—essentially the inverse of the steady, multiple-foci containment strategy authored by Kennan that outlasted the Soviet Union. If America lacked a strategy after the Cold War, this was Bush 43's answer. The problem was, its assumptions were almost all wrong. In the preamble to his National Security Strategy, Bush pledged that any decision for war would be reached only after "using the best intelligence and proceeding with deliberation." In this respect, what followed in Iraq was a violation of the president's own doctrine: the intelligence was far from good, and the process was anything but deliberate. But the drumbeat was becoming louder.

The White House pushed for a congressional vote authorizing force against Iraq during the month before the midterm elections. Democratic members with presidential aspirations, especially those in the Senate, would be put on the spot. A number who had voted against the 1991 Persian Gulf resolution—most notably Joe Biden and John Kerry—would ultimately authorize military action against Iraq the second time around. My constituents, as I told the *Los Angeles Times*, were "much more concerned about the potential suicide bomber next door than they are about what Saddam Hussein may have in store for us in a year or so when he gains nuclear capability." The government apparatus for securing the homeland was still a mess. As far as I was concerned, the homeland was still the main front against terrorism.

By then I was back on the HPSCI, having won back my seat and regained seniority just behind Pelosi, who was ranking member. Determined to get Iraq right, I did what had come naturally since my earlier days on the Hill: I went to school on the subject. Not only did I study the highly classified CIA analyses available to me as a member of the House Intelligence Committee, but I went to the United Kingdom to learn what their intelligence agencies had to say. The consensus was overwhelming—Iraq had the supplies and facilities to create biological and chemical weapons (and possibly radiological ones), and some delivery mechanisms. These could be easily transferred to nonstate groups to strike the U.S. homeland. With memories of 9/11 still fresh, the inclination of most of the Congress was to err on the side of assuming—imagining, even—too much rather than too little.

Iraq presented a conundrum. Saddam had started two

major wars, had attacked multiple neighbors (including Israel), and was a sworn enemy of the United States. For more than a decade intelligence agencies under the Clinton and both Bush administrations concluded that Iraq almost certainly had weapons and materials that could be used to attack the United States. A regional U.S. military buildup, bolstered by bipartisan support from the Congress, provided the best chance of forcing Saddam to disclose fully his clandestine weapons programs. It was also true that any military operation came with great risks—above all that troops might encounter a chemical gas attack as part of a last-ditch bid by Saddam to survive, though hopefully his generals would take things into their own hands at that point. The notion that Saddam would go to such lengths of obstruction as preventing U.N. inspectors' access to suspected weapons sites—and thus expose his country to suffering through international sanctions and war—for nonexistent weapons was unthinkable.

We knew deposing the regime meant that we would have to maintain a military presence in Iraq for a sustained period. And it would be expensive—costing billions of dollars, and possibly tens of billions. The administration and most of us in the Congress envisioned a postwar situation akin to that in the Balkans during the mid- to late 1990s. The stabilization phase would be mostly a peacekeeping operation, likely multilateral, using the United Nations and possibly NATO. The administration had been tight-lipped about post-regime plans. But the Bush team—the vice president, secretary of defense, and secretary of state—all had formidable national security chops (two of them had been secretaries of defense in earlier administrations, and a third had been chair of the Joint Chiefs) and reputations as strong managers.

The congressional resolution ultimately negotiated with the White House seemed like a reasonable compromise: the most bellicose language was deleted, and a reference to pursuing diplomacy at the UN was inserted. I told the media outlet *The Hill* that the new provisions addressed "many of my constituents' concerns, while also allowing us to address the clear and present threat posed by Saddam Hussein." This all might sound hopelessly naive and unrealistic, and indeed it turned out to be so. But it represented mainstream national security thinking by serious people at the time. (The far left and isolationist right predictably opposed any military engagement.)

However, not everyone in the establishment bought it. Former Bush 41 national security advisor Brent Scowcroft published an op-ed in the *Wall Street Journal* opposing a military invasion on the grounds it would destabilize the region and undermine the diplomatic and intelligence efforts against terrorism. He was promptly ostracized by the White House, and he was castigated, mocked even, in the conservative media as out of touch and burdened with a pre-9/11 mentality.

Another figure who did not agree with this view was Senate Intelligence Committee chair (until January 2003) Bob Graham, who represented Florida. Graham conceded the likely presence in Iraq of banned weapons. Although he had been one of only ten Democratic senators to vote in support of the Gulf War in 1991, he feared that using force against Iraq this time would cause the real war on terror—against Al Qaeda and its offshoots—to suffer as a result. Pro-Bush and pro-military sentiments were strong in Florida, but Graham bravely and presciently voted no.

One tragic figure in the lead-up to the vote in the Congress was House majority leader Dick Armey, a Texas Republican. Because he was one of the House's top Republicans, his support was assumed. However, Armey had his doubts from the outset, and when he was shown the National Intelligence Estimate (NIE) on Iraq, he was underwhelmed (as was Bush 43, thus prompting CIA director George Tenet to say, "Mr. President, it's a slam dunk"). As we would learn later, the sourcing for many NIE conclusions was unreliable and outdated—stretched to the most alarming possible interpretations. Cheney would eventually lobby Armey personally, showing him additional and more alarming Iraq material (later proved false). Armey's deep misgivings continued, but he felt he had no choice but to vote yes. We'll never know if a principled stand by a senior Republican—in the House, Armey was second only to the Speaker—could have slowed the rush to war.

As deputy secretary of defense Paul Wolfowitz reportedly said, the case for Iraq's weapons of mass destruction (WMD) was the one thing everyone could agree on—it could be sold to allies concerned about Iraq's perceived violation of multiple UN Security Council resolutions, it was frightening to the American public, and it was most convincing to members of Congress like me. However, those of us who weren't neoconservatives but still supported the Iraq War resolution failed to consider two core questions of strategy: What if all our assumptions—not just about WMD but also about the motivations of the Iraqi regime—were fundamentally wrong? And, more important, even if those assumptions were mostly right (if, say, stockpiles of chemical and biological weapons turned up), what next? As David Petraeus, at the time a major general, said, "Tell me how this ends." As we found out later with Afghanistan, whatever the merits of the initial intervention, once a war starts it has a way of perpetuating itself at enormous costs in ways far removed from its original purpose.

I had little interest in the grand designs of the Iraq War's most ardent supporters. My focus was on how Iraqi WMD could be used to harm the United States. I was impressed by the presentation by secretary of state Colin Powell to the UN Security Council. Shortly afterward I commented to CNN about Powell's speech: "I think the administration spent too many months using cowboy rhetoric and not enough months putting the facts out. . . . That's the right way to build support hopefully for peaceful disarmament in Iraq. . . . Doing nothing is the worst option at this point."

In the months that followed the quick regime change in Baghdad, no weapons of mass destruction were found and the growing insurgency foretold a long, bloody, and costly military campaign. I was encouraged when my friend and fellow commissioner Jerry Bremer was appointed to lead the Coalition Provisional Authority, or CPA (effectively making him the U.S. quasi-colonial viceroy of Iraq). Jerry would later get tarred with the disastrous decision to fire all Baath Party members from the Iraqi government and disband the Iraqi army—dismantling the last remaining cohesive (and respected) institution of Iraqi society. However, very little happened in Iraq without the approval of the Pentagon leadership: the secretary of defense, Donald Rumsfeld, and his lieutenants, deputy secretary Paul Wolfowitz and undersecretary of defense for policy Doug Feith. My law school friend Walter Slocombe was also involved in the CPA and had a major role in designing the de-Baathification policy.

My goal for Iraq during this period was minimal: to reverse a deteriorating situation on the ground, pride and ideals be damned. That meant honoring prewar construction contracts with Saddam Hussein's government held by France, Germany, and Russia. However, the Defense Department did the opposite—excluding countries that had opposed the war from bidding on huge infrastructure contracts. At that point, given the chaotic situation in Iraq and our failure to find weapons of mass destruction, the United States was in no position to lecture or alienate anyone. The fleeting opportunity to build a new strategy to confront shared threats had been lost.

In September I told CNN: "I want the president to tell us what's really in store for Americans. How much are we going to pay? What is the possible loss of life going forward? And how is he going to repair the damage to our relationship with international organizations, so that they step up and bear a reasonable share of this?" I later told the *Washington Post*, "There's no possible way that we can pay those costs in Iraq." Yet pay we would: first the $18 billion for Iraqi reconstruction requested by the administration that fall, and then in ever-increasing war-funding requests thereafter.

I never subscribed to the "Bush lied, people died" battle cry that became popular with many Democrats in the wake of the invasion. Senior leaders in the administration were sincere in their beliefs about Iraq's WMD program, and most of those beliefs—though not all—were supported by intelligence estimates provided by career professionals. But looking back, it became clear that claims about WMD were simply a means to a long-sought end. The more idealistic neoconservatives thought that a pro-Western democracy in Iraq would have a virtuous liberalizing domino effect throughout the region, crippling the appeal of extremists and even leading to a Palestinian-Israeli peace ("The road to Jerusalem goes through Baghdad" was the phrase used). Whatever the motivation and agenda, the most ardent supporters of regime change were going to have their war no matter what. And we in the Congress let them do it and in some cases helped them.

By 2007, more than 3,000 U.S. troops had been killed in Iraq, tens of thousands had been grievously wounded, and hundreds of billions of dollars had been spent. Iraqi losses and suffering were many times greater. For those of us old enough to remember Vietnam, it was like reliving a nightmare. A debate arose about adding 30,000 ground troops to Iraq (called the "surge"), a proposal championed by a new team including America's top diplomat, Ryan Crocker, and its savviest general, David Petraeus. I wrote: "A surge in troops may have been a great idea three and a half years ago but it makes no sense now. There is no way to achieve success in Iraq using military force. If, and it's a big if, stability can be achieved in Iraq, it will only be accomplished by getting buy-in of Sunnis, Shiites and Kurds and making certain that the government is strong enough to act. Neither of these conditions exists now." I endorsed the idea put forward by Les Gelb, past president of the Council on Foreign Relations, and Senator Joe Biden to create three autonomous regions inside the country for Sunnis, Shiites, and Kurds. I saw a glimmer of hope, strangely enough, in the Bosnia example. As I explained, "After brutal ethnic cleansing following the death of Tito, Yugoslavia separated. People now think of the Balkans as a reasonable success story or at least not a failure."

Later, after violence in Iraq declined dramatically, administration officials and senators including Lindsey Graham and John McCain would berate those like me who had opposed the surge. It certainly was far more successful militarily than prior performance in Iraq would have led us to expect (even its biggest supporters considered the surge a gamble). The surge bought some time and space for the Iraqi government to get its act together and for the different factions to reconcile. But that didn't happen. The collapse of Iraqi security forces in the face of an ISIS assault years later showed how shallow and fragile the progress was. It also showed how

stability depended on a large and open-ended U.S. presence
(McCain mentioned during his 2008 presidential run that it
might need to last "100 years")—a presence that would be un-
acceptable to most Americans and their elected representatives.
Iraq in the first decade of the twenty-first century was not
Germany or Japan after World War II, or Korea in the 1950s.

Barack Obama said when he ran for president in 2008
that he didn't just want to end the enormously unpopular
Iraq War, "but I want to end the mindset that got us into war
in the first place." That mindset was an inclination to use
military force—or other violent "kinetic" instruments, such
as targeted assassinations—as the principal means of dealing
with difficult security challenges. (Ironically, Obama himself
would succumb to this mindset on more than one occasion
after becoming president.)

One of the most cited, and politically most damning, arguments against U.S. military action in Iraq was that it fatally
undermined the "good war" in Afghanistan—the campaign
directly tied to the 9/11 attacks. During his presidential campaign Obama, trying to shore up his national defense bona
fides against a genuine war hero, John McCain, promised
to increase troops in Afghanistan as he withdrew from Iraq.
But in clamoring to give full attention to the "good war,"
too many leaders, Democrats especially, succumbed to the
same militarized instincts that got us into trouble in Iraq in
the first place. Because a significant increase in U.S. troops in
Iraq in 2007 dramatically lowered levels of violence through

the use of counterinsurgency tactics, it was tempting to believe another surge could do the same in Afghanistan. When
President Obama took office, he was trapped in two ways: by
his own campaign rhetoric and by the Pentagon top brass's
push for escalation.

The seven grim years since 9/11 had convinced me that
simply pouring more U.S. forces and massive aid projects into
these fractured societies was never going to work. In January
2009, before Obama's inauguration, I told CNN: "I don't
think inserting 30,000 troops or spending $30 billion to
$50 billion is going to turn the corner on this problem. . . .
What will turn the corner on this problem is if the Afghani
government cleans up its rampant corruption. . . . If they are
not willing to do it, and on present facts they are not willing
to do it, there's no way inserting any number of troops will
win any kind of victory there."

The original justification of the Afghanistan campaign
was to punish the perpetrators of 9/11 and their allies while
ensuring the country would not become an Al Qaeda sanc-
tuary again. But since that time the nature of the terror threat
had changed under our noses. The main terrorist threat
to the U.S. homeland had morphed from a centralized Al
Qaeda into a loose horizontal affiliation of groups in Yemen,
in the Horn of Africa, and in Iraq after the U.S. invasion.
Sending tens of thousands more troops—the total number
would reach more than 100,000 at the height of the Afghan
surge—did little to address the evolving terrorist threat to
Americans at home. A bigger military footprint in Afghanistan might have been stabilizing in the first years after the

Taliban fled, and perhaps might even have made a lasting difference. But not later.

I was not willing to write off Afghanistan. The United States could not afford a humiliating defeat there, something akin to the chaotic helicopter evacuation of Saigon in 1975. Millions of girls and women had begun attending school and were joining Afghan civic life in ways forbidden under the Taliban (though the harshest sharia rules and punishments still held sway in parts of the country). I was not on the House committees—Armed Services, Foreign Affairs, or (after 2006) HPSCI—with direct oversight of the Afghan campaign. But I kept well informed from a variety of official and unofficial sources. One of the latter was an extraordinary woman named Sarah Chayes. She first went to Afghanistan as a reporter for NPR, then led an aid project in Kandahar, and eventually became a civilian advisor to the chair of the Joint Chiefs of Staff. Sarah also happened to be the daughter of my Harvard Law School mentor, Abram Chayes, one of the leading international lawyers of his generation. Her mother, Antonia Handler Chayes, an impressive lawyer in her own right, was the first woman undersecretary of the air force, a post she held during the Carter administration. Unlike other Western reporters and aid workers, Sarah lived and worked directly with the Afghan people in a women-run cooperative. She had no security detail. Feeling much affection (and responsibility) toward her family, I was worried about what might happen to her—a kidnapping for ransom, or worse. I'll never forget visiting her during one of my trips to Afghanistan. We sat around with some of the village elders.

Sarah, who spoke Pashtu fluently, was the translator when I asked the elders if she was safe in their community. With some umbrage, they told me that Sarah was their "sister" and would be protected. Still, it was reported that Sarah slept with a Kalashnikov rifle by her bed for a couple of years.

Sarah's experiences on the ground outside the bubble of the capital, Kabul, provided unique insight into the biggest enemy in Afghanistan: not the forces of the Taliban, as dangerous and vicious as they could be, but corruption. Average Afghans had such terrible experiences dealing with the government at the local, provincial, and national levels that they felt little allegiance to their leaders. Sarah spent a fair amount of time around the ruling Karzai family, and she saw them receive packages of $100 bills from the CIA. They and other Afghan elites eventually received billions of dollars of Western largesse, much of it spent on lavish mansions (de facto escape pods) in the United Arab Emirates and other Gulf monarchies.

A decade and thousands of American casualties later, we are still in Afghanistan, albeit in vastly reduced numbers. The Trump administration has negotiated a "peace deal" with the Taliban, and the numbers of U.S. troops are being further reduced. Many, including me, are skeptical that this deal will succeed.

Other Obama military interventions would follow the Afghanistan surge—first in the skies over Libya to depose Muammar Gaddafi, then in Iraq and Syria to beat back ISIS. Though each operation had some merit, the cumulative outcome was more use of U.S. military force to address what are fundamentally political problems in the Middle East—between Sunnis and Shiites, between Islamists and secularists, between authoritarians and democrats. During the 2010s, which turned out to be another lost decade, other important U.S. interests and instruments of U.S. power continued to be shortchanged. The Obama administration later pledged to pivot toward Asia and away from the focus on terrorism, but the cycle of military involvement in the Middle East—a geopolitical version of the interminably repeating events in the film *Groundhog Day*—would continue. President Trump came to office pledging to stop the "endless wars." Instead, his impulsive, process-free approach—pulling U.S. forces from Syria without consulting allies, ordering the drone assassination of a top Iranian military leader—only created more instability.

The return to "great power competition" with Russia and China—as stated in the Pentagon's 2018 National Defense Strategy[3]—has been the justification for another surge in defense spending. The regions and adversaries may change, as do the weapons and equipment, but the milita-

---

3 The NDS issued by the secretary of defense is supposed to reflect the military implications of the broader National Security Strategy, which was issued by the White House in December 2017.

rized character of American statecraft does not. I've seen the Pentagon—with firm support from the Congress—continue to spend astronomical sums on conventional weapons systems, including fighter jets, bombers, helicopters, and large surface ships. The air force's biggest procurement priority in recent years has been the F-35 Joint Strike Fighter, which will cost approximately $400 billion to buy and hundreds of billions more to operate. The U.S. Navy's most sacrosanct program is the *Ford*-class aircraft carrier, averaging $10 to $15 billion *per ship* (not counting the air wing).

There is no shortage of smart, visionary people in our military who could reimagine and redesign defense spending. The question is whether the White House or the Congress will let them. For example, the Defense Advanced Research Projects Agency (DARPA) has developed an underwater drone that can operate for sixty to ninety days at a small fraction of the cost of a conventional crewed attack submarine. The new chief of naval operations has advocated for a more realistic and affordable mix of crewed warships and autonomous vessels such as ACTUV and the Optical RF Communications Adjunct (ORCA).

There is a U.S. Air Force–led effort to connect all defense platforms over one digital network. The network would allow the various branches of the military to constantly share, sort, and analyze information about enemy threats, new targets, friendly movements, the weather, or anything else relevant to modern combat. Putting the network together and then keeping it secure from hacking or jamming is a huge technological challenge. This new project is being met with skepticism, even fear, in parts of the Pentagon and Congress because it would shift the emphasis (and some funding) away from crewed aircraft to the new network.

In the past, government-funded R&D would fuel innovation in the commercial space (two good examples are the internet and satellite navigation). My priority in the 1990s was getting traditional defense contractors to adapt their skill sets and product lines for "dual use" products. Today, technologies with military applications may start out in the commercial tech sector and be repurposed for defense. Internet giants are becoming defense and intelligence contractors (Amazon for cloud hosting, Microsoft for high-tech combat goggles). The Air Force and National Geospatial-Intelligence Agency leadership rely on inexpensive commercial satellites—some as small as 100 pounds—instead of billion-dollar purpose-built military satellites.

Given the pace of technological change, we can no longer spend ten to twenty years developing major weapons systems that may be obsolete by the time they are produced. This is where Congress—or its authorizing committees, anyway—has been helpful in providing new "rapid acquisition" authorities. These allow the military to skip the usual steps and acquire prototypes, "fail fast" if need be, and continuously upgrade. The Pentagon is getting on board, but the habits of risk aversion—no one wants to see another headline about $800 toilet seats—die hard within the acquisition bureaucracies.

Getting the military right-sized and buying the right things does not address the more fundamental shortcomings of U.S. statecraft. In many cases, they reach back to the end of the Cold War. During the 1990s, the U.S. Foreign Service stopped hiring new officers, and the U.S. Information Agency, which was responsible for public diplomacy, was folded into the State Department. Budgets for diplomacy increased after 9/11—though not nearly at the scale of defense and intelligence budgets. But much of this new funding was consumed by security requirements in Iraq, Afghanistan, and other unstable posts like Libya. The Trump administration slashed these important "soft power" functions. Also absent was fresh thinking. The State Department personnel system is designed principally to staff embassies, and since the end of the Cold War there are now many more of them. America will always need foreign missions and talented diplomats to staff them. But many of the most relevant bilateral and international interactions are taking place outside official channels through commercial, research, social, and cultural exchanges between nongovernment groups and persons, many of them online. Various attempts at bringing public diplomacy into the twenty-first century—in particular, the Global Engagement Center, whose task is to counter disinformation by everyone from ISIS to the Russians—have had mixed success. Ultimately the real war on terror will be won in the hearts and minds of young people across the world, Muslim and otherwise. For too long their views of what America stands for have been distorted by a succession of U.S. military actions (including drone strikes).

In many respects we've come full circle. Nearly twenty years ago, America's formidable conventional war machine could do little to prevent a handful of radicalized militants using box cutters from bringing our country to a standstill. In 2020, after trillions of dollars in military expenditures and multiple wars, a virus originating in a Chinese "wet market" inflicted even more economic and human damage. Overcoming the most lethal threats of the twenty-first century—at least those threats that pose the greatest risk to the health and well-being of the average citizen—will require staying the itchy trigger finger of militarized statecraft. Ultimately, achieving true security will require embracing a broader "whole of government" and "whole of nation" set of tools that reflects the full strength of America.

TWO

The Threats Keep Evolving
and We're Still Unprepared

In August 2001, eight months after returning to the Congress, I held a forum at the National Guard Armory in Manhattan Beach. It was to discuss the need for a new counterterrorism training and command center in Los Angeles. I had requested $2 million to implement a network that would better link Los Angeles County's eighty-eight municipalities in the event of a disaster. Good parochial politics, yes, but also good policy. Speaking to a group of state, local, and federal officials, I said: "This threat is more real, more immediate and potentially more damaging to U.S. citizens than ballistic missiles or regional conflicts on the other side of the globe." At the time, ballistic missile defense was shaping up to be the top national defense priority of the new Bush administration. National security advisor Condoleezza Rice was scheduled to give a speech on September 11, 2001, on "the threats and problems of today and the day after, not the world of yesterday," according to excerpts of the prepared text later obtained by the *Washington Post*. The principal topic of the speech was ballistic missile defense. To the extent terrorism was discussed, it dwelled on sponsorship by rogue states such as Iraq and North Korea. Al Qaeda did not merit a mention. Nor did Osama Bin Laden or violent Islamic extremism generally.

On September 10, 2001, when Jerry Bremer and I had lunch at the Red River Grill near Union Station in Washington, D.C., we bemoaned the fact that, despite broad dissemination of and congressional testimony about our commission's recommendations on how to address international terrorism, no one was paying attention. Twenty-four hours later, they surely were.

This chapter explains how after two decades and the creation of several huge new government bureaucracies, the lack of strategic focus on protecting the homeland persists even as asymmetric threats evolve and increase.

That the U.S. government had so badly underestimated—underimagined, really—what Al Qaeda could do and was willing to do on 9/11 immediately raised the question of what else we had missed and what might be coming next. The CIA and FBI believed it quite possible that a second wave of attacks was coming, possibly within days. "They aren't convinced it is over," I told the *Washington Post* shortly after the attack. The reports by the Bremer Commission and the Hart-Rudman Commission were dusted off and read with new purpose. Both warned about terrorists using unsecured chemical, biological, or nuclear materials to launch a mass-casualty attack (the soon-to-be-infamous phrase "weapons of mass destruction" was not in common parlance yet). "Bad guys are capable of developing these agents, but they are not very capable of delivering them," I said on CNN in late September. "What is new is the wanton destruction of September 11 makes clear there would be no hesitation against using them." Right on cue, envelopes containing anthrax spores appeared in members' offices on Capitol Hill. I thought it might have been a lone jihadist taking cues from Bin Laden. A highly respected former UN weapons inspector, Richard Butler, speculated publicly that the anthrax might have come from Iraq. The FBI later came to suspect a domestic source.

The Bremer Commission had already identified significant shortcomings in America's intelligence and law enforcement agencies: risk aversion at the CIA, following alleged human rights abuses by former assets in Central America, which hindered the recruitment of terrorist informants; excessive FBI restraint when it came to its domestic security responsibilities, including an overly strict view of what was permitted in terms of searches and wiretaps; a legal "wall" to protect defendants and sources that hindered cooperation between the intelligence community and domestic law enforcement; lack of mechanisms for sharing information across the intelligence community, the Justice Department, and the rest of the government at all levels; a student visa program rife with room for abuse; and much more that would be revealed, in infuriating detail, after the fact.

Up to that point the suspected perpetrators of terror attacks had been pursued, indicted, convicted, and incarcerated. The emphasis was on investigation and punishment—two functions squarely within the FBI's wheelhouse—rather than prevention. Our commission looked at how other countries had approached the same challenge. The United States was unique in not having a ministry or organization devoted to domestic security, such as the United Kingdom's Home Office and MI5. After World War II, FBI director J. Edgar Hoover and the American Civil Liberties Union (ACLU) joined forces—for the first and probably only time—to prevent the establishment of such an agency: the ACLU for obvious reasons, Hoover to make sure that this mission remained within the FBI's purview.

The most controversial aspect of our commission's report was a recommendation to track the visa status of foreign students studying at American institutions of higher education. Advocacy groups for colleges and universities howled. Others took issue with our recommendation for a greater—though still limited—role for the U.S. military domestically in response to a mass-scale terrorist attack (which was consistent with the oft-cited but rarely understood Posse Comitatus Act). Both objections were quickly forgotten after the World Trade Center towers came down.

I had returned to the Congress as the only sitting member to have served on one of the major pre-9/11 terrorism commissions. Upon taking office in January 2001 I was appointed co-chair of the newly formed Speaker's Working Group on International Terrorism and Homeland Security, tasked by Speaker Dennis Hastert to take a holistic look at U.S. government readiness. In keeping with the political priorities of the time, the panel was not one of the 100 official subcommittees in the House.

In the summer of 2001 the working group scheduled a field hearing to be held in the autumn at the World Trade Center to talk about facilities protection, emergency response, and information sharing in the wake of a potential terrorist attack. At the end of October our subcommittee went ahead with the hearing at City Hall in downtown Manhattan, blocks from where the towers had fallen. On that trip, we also visited the 9/11 site—which still housed a trailer morgue. Tragically, one of the witnesses scheduled to appear had died in the attacks seven weeks earlier. Testifying at our hearing, New York City mayor Rudy Giuliani proposed that Congress pass a law requiring the FBI and other federal authorities to do a better job of sharing intelligence with local police and government officials. Given what had just happened, it seemed strange, almost obscene, that it might require legislation to make this happen. "Do we really need to pass a law?" I asked. "Couldn't the director of the FBI just start doing that?" Giuliani, a former U.S. attorney who, back then, was a stickler for legality, replied: "You need to legislate permission to do that."

Partisanship was shelved for at least a little while in the wake of 9/11. But there were pointed and increasingly angry questions about how such an attack could have happened. "The blame game doesn't fix the problem," I commented. "Protecting against the next waves is job No. 1, job No. 2 and job No. 3." Yet at some point there would need to be an investigation and a full accounting. Talk of an independent commission to investigate began almost as soon as the twin towers fell. John McCain proposed bringing back Warren

Rudman and Gary Hart to head up a blue-ribbon group. From my perspective, this was squarely within the Article I responsibility of the Congress, and within the jurisdiction of the intelligence committees.

An unclassified summary of our subcommittee's findings was released in July 2002 and, unsurprisingly, reflected many of the gaps identified previously by the terrorism commissions. We found that the CIA put out so much information, much of it vague, that U.S. domestic agencies had difficulty determining how to respond. The FBI's decentralized structure plus its outdated and incompatible information technology systems hindered its counterterrorism efforts. The Bureau's organizational culture focused on investigating crimes, not preventing attacks—a function of its origins and of its most celebrated success, which had come fighting the Mafia.

Nine months after 9/11, the White House was claiming that bipartisan congressional investigations—including Congress's joint inquiry, which combined the House and Senate intelligence committees and provided equal roles for both the minority and majority parties (its full formal name was the Joint Inquiry into Intelligence Community Activities Before and After the Terrorist Attacks of September 11, 2001)—would needlessly divert the government from the task at hand. I had bent over backward to be supportive, whenever possible, of the administration's counterterror efforts. Beyond a certain point, however, the foot-dragging on accountability and structural change was starting to grate. As I commented, "I want to understand what went wrong . . .

what was broken in the system so we can fix it, but the goal is to fix the system."

President Bush acknowledged that communications between the CIA and FBI had broken down, but he said he was aware of "no evidence" that the government could have prevented the attacks. It would soon become clear why the White House was wary of a thorough (and public) inquiry. During these months, Americans learned about the proverbial dots that had been left unconnected: different parts of the government had had relevant pieces of information, but no one had put them together. Many of the missing or ignored signals preceded the Bush administration, but the president and his national security team still had a good deal to answer for.

Among the most infuriating revelations was a May 2002 memorandum sent by FBI agent Coleen Rowley. It described how superiors had ignored reports by the Minneapolis field office about a suspected Al Qaeda operative—Zacarias Moussaoui, the would-be twentieth hijacker—taking classes at a flight school. Rowley was scheduled to appear before the Senate Judiciary Committee on June 6, 2002. However, her searing testimony was not the lead item on the evening news. That was the day, conveniently for the administration, that the White House announced the biggest reorganization of the U.S. government in more than half a century.

The administration's June 2002 proposal—in reality, its begrudging concession—to create a cabinet-level Department of Homeland Security followed nine months of slow-rolling

the Congress. From the start it was clear that information
sharing among agencies should be, as I put it, "the crux of
any homeland security effort." Rampant over-classification
of documents and information at the federal level restricted
what could be shared with the state and local agencies that
would be the first to respond. These challenges cut very close
to home. My district included the contiguous ports of Los
Angeles and Long Beach, which received nearly 6,000 large
vessels each year. Through the ports moved several million
containers with bulk goods, plus billions of gallons of potentially toxic and explosive petroleum products and chemicals.
Communication was critical. I spent several hours on September 11 anxiously trying to reach my youngest daughter,
then at a D.C. high school, by phone. She was safe, but the
cell tower system in Washington had crashed due to overuse.
That made clear to me that emergency responders needed
interoperable equipment with dedicated channels free from
commercial and personal traffic.

Shortly after the attacks the White House appointed
Pennsylvania governor Tom Ridge as director of homeland
security. He was charged with leading and coordinating all
the activities—state, local, federal—necessary to prevent another terror attack on U.S. soil. A much-admired moderate
Republican who had served in Vietnam as an infantry ser-
geant, Ridge was the embodiment of public-mindedness and
common decency. From the start, I wanted him to be more
assertive in public as the clear and only face of the government response. Too often some combination of the attorney
general, FBI director, and other federal leaders rushed to the

microphone after the latest terror scare. I wanted Ridge to be the "C. Everett Koop of Homeland Security," emulating the former health official who was widely respected when he demonstrated the harms of smoking. Ridge got off to a rocky start with his color-coded warning system, which provided little useful information to the average person. At one point the threat advisory was raised from "pale yellow" to "dark yellow," and I asked in a hearing if Ridge was secretary of homeland security or an interior decorator. Tom was a good sport—I got a call from him shortly thereafter asking if I needed any help decorating my kitchen.

As a former governor, Ridge had great rapport with state and local officials. He recognized intuitively that "homeland security is hometown security": though terrorism was a federal responsibility, it would be police and firefighters who would be the first to respond. The real problem, evident almost from the first day, was that Ridge lacked enough real power—above all, authority over budget and personnel—to do what needed to be done. Representatives of federal agencies would come to his meetings and read his memos, but their real boss was a cabinet secretary who reported to various congressional committees. So it would be impossible to win the war on terror without first winning the "war on turf."

That fall I led a bipartisan effort to give Ridge clear budget authority over anti-terrorism functions. Initially the White House was firmly opposed to creating a Senate-confirmed position, much less a new cabinet department. Press secretary Ari Fleischer proclaimed that legislation was "just not necessary." From the White House perspective, a cabinet department would be accountable to the Congress in ways that presidential appointees were not.

There was a growing disconnect between the administration's focus and the resources dedicated to the military and intelligence campaign overseas and to measures to improve protections at home. "The administration has pursued a clear and committed war strategy against the Taliban regime and al-Qaida. But our homeland security strategy, which may affect millions more Americans, has been ad hoc, inconsistent and confusing," I said at the time.

No matter how effective our military, how connected our proverbial dots, or how prescient our intelligence agencies, it would be impossible to prevent every terrorist from getting into the country and conducting some kind of attack. The United States was confronted with an asymmetric dilemma: we have to be right 100 percent of the time, but the terrorist only has to be right once. So I was all for fighting the "away game," focusing on threats we could identify outside our nation's borders. But we needed an equally effective—arguably, more effective—"home game" as well.

In his State of the Union address at the end of January 2002, Bush referred to maps and diagrams of American nuclear power and water supply plants that had been recovered in Afghanistan, suggesting that Al Qaeda was at least considering attacks on those facilities. A comprehensive, threat-based homeland security strategy was promised—sometime later in the year. It was Bush's proclamation of the "Axis of Evil" that grabbed the headlines. Iran, Iraq, and North Korea did pose threats and would need to be dealt with. But most Americans were worried about being blown up or poisoned in their homes, in their workplaces, on the subway, or, as on 9/11, in an attack we had never imagined.

A few days after the State of the Union speech, President Bush submitted a budget request reflecting his policy priorities, including $38 billion for homeland security. The budget boosted border security, bioterrorism defenses, first responders, and information sharing. It did not sufficiently address intelligence, critical infrastructure, or defense against cyberattacks and crude nuclear devices (so-called dirty bombs).

Ultimately, the problem was that we had an administration in search of a strategy. I wrote: "Our nation cannot afford to go from event to event and crisis to crisis. Our governors, our mayors and our first responders are crying out for a clearly defined national strategy to rely on for guidance." The obsession with preventing another 9/11—focusing on aviation to the exclusion of other vulnerabilities—was akin to refighting the last war. It would repeat the mistake made in defense planning during the 1990s by continuing to invest in a Cold War–style military (albeit smaller) against a set of threats that ultimately did not look anything like the Soviet Union.

By then Tom Ridge's staff had grown nearly tenfold and he had improved as a communicator. But the federal agencies and departments were getting less responsive as 9/11 grew more distant in the rearview mirror. When the military suspended air patrols over New York, Ridge was only informed after the fact. One senior assistant to the secretary of defense, reflecting the sentiments of his boss, was bold enough to be quoted by name telling the news media: "We don't tell the Office of Homeland Security about recommendations, only about decisions." Other cabinet secretaries would rush out with announcements on terrorism-related topics that were supposed to be in Ridge's new portfolio.

When asked about the snubs, Ridge said he would accept more authority but that his current role was to be a coordinator and enabler for federal, state, and local officials: "We're not Pac-Man trying to gobble up power, money and responsibility," he told the *New York Times*. Nor would the White House let him testify formally before Congress. Instead, an event was held in one of the Capitol's most ornate reception rooms, in which Ridge gave a briefing and took questions from a handful of Republican senators (it was open to Democrats as well, but we refused to attend what we considered a glorified press conference).

Ridge attempted to bring some cohesion to one part of the homeland security mission by proposing to consolidate several of the federal agencies dealing in some fashion with border control. Here he ran into opposition not only from the other departments but from the congressional committees that could lose jurisdiction. After being overruled by Bush, Ridge released a diluted border security proposal.

Six months after 9/11, much of the U.S. government still had not connected the dots. Suspected terrorists could appear on an Immigration and Naturalization Service (INS) watch list—as had happened before 9/11—without the FBI being aware of it. The State Department could still issue visas overseas without knowing if the applicant was on a CIA or FBI list. As Jerry Bremer told *USA Today* in May 2002: "Americans would be surprised to know there isn't a single list of bad guys that Americans can refer to."

Congress had had enough. Some of us had been beating the drum for months. The bill I had co-sponsored in November with Nevada Republican Jim Gibbons was still on the table. It would have created a cabinet-level position, subject to Senate confirmation, with the responsibility to create and execute national strategy for homeland security and direct information sharing between intelligence agencies and law enforcement. In May, I would team up with Texas Republican Mac Thornberry to introduce legislation creating a new homeland security department. I said when announcing the bill: "No organization guarantees failure—and we have had no organization."

The White House for months had resisted any serious reform, but it faced a more anxious electorate in advance of the 2002 midterm elections. And we were all about to hear the most damning 9/11 testimony yet, by the FBI's Rowley. That was when the White House made a 180-degree turn and proposed a new Department of Homeland Security that was much bigger (170,000 employees) and encompassed a wider range of agencies (twenty-two) than anything suggested before. Given the magnitude of the administration's proposal, it was clear that it had been in the works for a long time (since April, it turned out). When asked about the timing, White House chief of staff Andy Card said, "Why now? Because it's ready now," to incredulity in the media and on the Hill.

The idea of merging so many agencies into one department did not go over well with many members of Congress. Especially irked were the chairs of committees and subcommittees with jurisdiction over departments that would be losing high-profile functions (for example, the Secret Service was to be moved from the Treasury Department to the new Department of Homeland Security). There was also significant opposition by Democrats to parts of the White House proposal that, in the name of providing more flexibility for hiring and firing, would weaken civil service protections for employees in the new department. I shared these concerns but wanted to focus on the issues on which we could reach bipartisan agreement. In late September 2002 I co-authored an op-ed with Tom Ridge published in the *San Diego Union-Tribune* supporting the compromise language that had been hammered out. "The early debate threatened to disintegrate into a series of ugly turf battles," we wrote. "But when the dust settled, partisanship was put aside. The only turf we worried about protecting was the turf we stand on."

In addition to redrawing org charts, the legislation directed how elements of this new department would connect with other agencies and layers at each level of government: more information sharing, mutual assistance agreements, interoperable communications, risk-based infrastructure protections, intelligence fusion, and private-sector engagement. The resulting bill was far from ideal from my perspective and certainly that of many other Democrats. But as I pointed out to critics, even though the 1947 National Security Act had been far from perfect as well, it had proven to be a vital component of America's success in the Cold War.

Typically a president's party loses seats in the first midterm following a presidential election. But in November 2002 the Republicans won enough elections for a Senate majority. At that point congressional Democrats recognized that the bill I had helped negotiate with the White House was about the best we were going to get before the Republicans took control of both houses of Congress in January. "Finally, we will have a strategy to protect the homeland," I said—too optimistically, in retrospect. "This is the beginning of the solution to homeland vulnerability."

Even with maximum presidential support and under the best of circumstances, the process of standing up such an organization would have been a herculean task. But the existence of the Department of Homeland Security (DHS) was already a grudging concession by the White House, and this was reflected in the second-class treatment DHS received after it was formally established.

In May 2003 the White House debuted the Terrorist Threat Integration Center (TTIC), an independent organization bringing together representatives and information from the intelligence community, law enforcement, and homeland security agencies. The 9/11 Commission later

recommended putting a TTIC-like organization in the
new Department of Homeland Security (as did I). Its focus, after all, was primarily to connect domestic agencies
and law enforcement to avoid another failure. But when
intelligence reform was enacted at the end of 2004, these
functions were folded into the National Counter-Terrorism
Center (NCTC), which had been established by executive
order several months earlier and which reported to the
new director of national intelligence. I visited NCTC soon
thereafter and saw as many as seven different digital communications systems under each desk. We had a long way
to go.

The department's leadership faced a steep learning
curve. Tom Ridge's successor as secretary of homeland security, former assistant attorney general and federal judge
Michael Chertoff, was brilliant and a genuine strategic
thinker. He professionalized the department, created Centers of Excellence around the country to focus on hard
technical problems, and dramatically improved port and
airport security. But the department's handling of Hurricane Katrina was a fiasco. In an interview shortly after Katrina I said the federal government's failures had
"grave implications" for our ability to deal with terrorism. I couldn't help but think how the devastation in New
Orleans "resembles the detonation of a weapon of mass
destruction in a major American city." The White House
had earlier deemed NCTC too important to put it in
the Department of Homeland Security. After Katrina
many in the Congress thought the same about FEMA,

which had been incorporated into DHS when the department was established in 2003, and for a time considered returning it to being an independent federal agency. Subsequently, FEMA's performance improved and it remains part of DHS.

Despite the formation of homeland security committees in both houses, DHS leaders seeking funding and new policy authority were forced to make the rounds of other committees that still retained jurisdiction over agencies within the department. An effective congressional oversight structure would remain a key recommendation of the 9/11 Commission that went unheeded.

I would have the opportunity to have a more direct impact on domestic readiness after becoming chair of the Homeland Security Subcommittee on Intelligence, Information Sharing, and Terrorism Risk Assessment in January 2007. By then, the terrorist threat was evolving. As the United States ramped up drone killings of Al Qaeda leaders in Pakistan, increasing numbers of young Muslim men living in the United States and Europe, in many cases citizens of those Western countries, became radicalized. They used online publications and videos to train themselves and to learn how to build weapons (such as the pressure-cooker bombs used years later in the Boston Marathon attack). We would learn they could cause plenty of damage using available implements of modern life—from trucks to kitchen knives to (at least in America) assault rifles.

For years I had worried that the Port of Los Angeles would be either the target of a major attack or a conduit for destructive material used in an attack elsewhere. It turned out one of the most prominent cases of homegrown terrorism occurred in the city of Torrance, located in my district. There, in September 2005, officials disrupted the first known prison-based terror cell in the United States, consisting of three American citizens and one permanent resident who had been born in Pakistan. They were charged with having planned attacks on synagogues, U.S. military installations, and armed forces recruitment centers, with the planning directed by one of the men while he was still in prison and funded by eleven gas station robberies committed by the three who were on the outside. After the arrests of the four, the Torrance Police Department found maps and other evidence of plots under way, all of which was promptly shared with the Los Angeles police, the FBI, and Homeland Security. After taking over the subcommittee I brought the members to my district to see what lessons we could apply from the Torrance case.

In August 2007 two University of South Florida engineering students were stopped for speeding in South Carolina. When questioned by federal agents, they admitted to using the internet to post a twelve-minute YouTube video in Arabic demonstrating how to turn a toy boat into a bomb. A *New York Times* article a few months later introduced Samir Khan, a twenty-one-year-old American blogger operating from his parents' house in North Carolina. Khan ran a popular English-language website promoting radical Islam and violence against Americans. The site posted hundreds of links to videos showing American soldiers being killed in Iraq. Khan wrote in the comments: "You can even see an American soldier hiding during the ambush like a baby. Allah Akbar! Allah Akbar!"

From the outset I stressed that we should not target people from any particular ethnic, political, or religious group. Adam Gadahn was a Jewish kid living in Santa Ana, California. At age seventeen he became radicalized, moved to Pakistan, and went to work as Osama Bin Laden's spokesman (Gadahn was eventually killed in a 2015 U.S. drone strike). Then there was Hassan Abujihaad, a former U.S. Navy sailor and convert to Islam who was convicted in 2008 of having posted the location of navy ships years earlier with advice on how to attack them.

Responding to these developments, I introduced the Violent Radicalization and Homegrown Terrorism Prevention Act. The bill was modest in scope, creating a multidisciplinary commission and focusing on intervention at the point when the expression of radical beliefs, which is protected by the First Amendment, turns into violent action. My House colleagues were overwhelmingly in favor of it, voting 404–6 (those voting yes included virtually all progressive Democrats). As the action moved to the Senate, a few privacy groups that had been consulted previously suddenly decided that the bill created "thought crimes." In October 2007 a blogger posted an item titled "Jane Harman's War on the First Amendment." One ACLU official put out a statement recommending changes to the bill, only to conclude that the organization's support even of a changed bill was still unlikely because it involved "speech and belief." As it turned out, many of the ACLU-suggested changes had already been incorporated into the bill. In multiple hearings we had made clear that "radical speech" would continue to be protected under the Constitution, though incitements to violence would not be. After the House vote, Susan Collins took the lead in the effort to get the legislation through the Senate. It seemed like a no-brainer. But a flurry of online protests, petitions, and lobbying by "netroots" activists and others doomed the bill. It died without a Senate hearing.

In the ensuing years America would be horrified by the sight of jihadist-inspired U.S. citizens slaughtering their compatriots in Fort Hood, Boston, San Bernardino, Orlando, and New York. It's uncertain whether our legislation might have helped prevent these incidents. But the law would have provided more insight into how people become violent extremists and more tools to prevent these kinds of attacks. The failure to do so triggered far more anti-Islamic sentiment in the United States. The stage was set for a major-party presidential candidate to campaign in 2016 on imposing a "Muslim ban."

Domestic terror plots underscored the importance of information sharing—not the most scintillating of topics, but arguably the principal difference between stopping an attack and letting it happen. There had been promising improvement in the sharing of information at the state and local levels, largely because these levels of government had taken the initiative to develop intelligence fusion centers. The centers, staffed by police and sheriff's officers, public health authorities, and many others, including from the private sector, represented a response from the ground up. These local initiatives were encouraging but raised the question of why more wasn't being done at the federal level. I took the subcommittee on the road and visited fusion centers in Los Angeles, Seattle, Denver, and Baltimore. We made sure that the 2007 legislation implementing the recommendations of the 9/11 Commission included tools for DHS to partner more effectively with these centers without dictating how they should be run.

The 9/11 attacks highlighted the gaps in "horizontal" information sharing—that is, among different agencies of the federal government (FBI, CIA, Border Patrol, INS, etc.). Our subcommittee also kept running into the barriers to "vertical" information sharing—among different layers within agencies and between levels of government. In combating homegrown threats, the front line against terrorism isn't necessarily a CIA operative undercover abroad, but perhaps a cop on a routine patrol who notices something odd going on, or a private citizen seeing something strange in the house next door. We needed to make sure that these folks knew what to look for and whom to share it with.

Unfortunately, many fusion centers were little more than co-location centers. Personnel from different agencies and levels of government were working in physical proximity to one another, but that was about as far as it went. I was especially baffled as to why DHS and the FBI still had not consolidated their databases. Fusion center staff often needed to log onto as many as five different networks to determine the threats they were waking up to each morning.

The "war on turf" never ended, and the Department of Homeland Security was usually on the losing side. It was still a new agency and somewhat of a neglected stepchild of the federal government. A major boost to DHS's clout arrived in the form of Charles Allen, a longtime CIA veteran whom one colleague called a "pile driver" for his insistence on going deeper for information. Allen became DHS's intelligence chief, working tirelessly to improve the agency's analytical function, to provide better support to the fusion centers, and to create new units that studied homegrown terrorism and border security issues. He also became a friend.

Every time one barrier to information sharing was addressed (or at least mitigated), another cropped up. One persistent issue was over-classification, which resulted in important information not reaching the people who needed to see it for lack of a security clearance. The 9/11 Commission cited over-classification as a major problem, but the government was moving in the opposite direction: between 2001 and 2005, the number of classification actions jumped from 8 million to 14 million. Much of this could be explained by the major increase in military operations and intelligence activities. Less justified was the steep decrease in declassification— from 100 million pages in 2001 to less than 30 million in 2005. There was also a proliferation of what I called pseudo-classifications: documents marked "protective," "sensitive," or "for official use only." These designations—less restrictive than "secret"—were enough to keep information from being shared within different layers of government. A case in point was a survey that DHS conducted in November 2006 titled "Special Assessment: Radicalization in the State of California." It was marked "unclassified, for official use only," and carried a disclaimer indicating that it could not be released to the public, the media, or other personnel without prior approval of an authorized DHS official. Ahead of our field hearing in Torrance the next year, my staff requested—and was denied—approval to release the survey results. They then asked for a redacted version of the document so that we could use at least some of its contents at the hearing. DHS was unable to provide one.

The tone on secrecy came from the very top. In July 2007 we learned that Vice President Dick Cheney's staff had been coming up with new variations of classified and unclassified designations to keep his work products away from other parts of the government, as well as the public. My personal favorite—one I had never come across during eight years on HPSCI—was "treated as: top secret/SCI." SCI, or "sensitive compartmentalized information," was the designation for the most closely guarded government secrets, revelation of which would cause "exceptionally grave damage to national security"; it was applied to things like covert intelligence actions or nuclear and missile defense technology. DHS had developed a category called CUI, or "controlled unclassified information," for information that could be shared within layers of government but not necessarily released to the public.

But with the example set by the White House, there was little hope that the CUI designation would become widely adopted. After multiple hearings it was clear the executive branch would not fix itself. "The out-of-control practice of classifying and reclassifying everything that moves is pernicious," I said in a hearing. "The local cop on the beat, who during his or her day-to-day work is most likely to uncover and foil a terrorist plot, isn't getting necessary information."

The subcommittee's ranking member, Dave Reichert, had been a sheriff's deputy, later sheriff of King County in Washington State, during the twenty-year-long investigation to find the Green River Killer. Reichert described an instance when he and an FBI agent had jointly interviewed a witness for that investigation. Reichert later asked the FBI for a copy of the agent's interrogation report so that he could compare notes. Despite the report having little bearing on national security—and despite the fact that Reichert had been there during the interrogation—the report was classified, so his request was denied. I enjoyed a good working relationship with Reichert and with most of the subcommittee's other Republicans during my tenure as chair. It harked back to the productive output of the Speaker's Working Group on International Terrorism and Homeland Security (which later became a formal subcommittee) before and after 9/11. In some respects our subcommittee had replaced HPSCI as the House's last bastion of bipartisan sanity.

Reichert and I introduced a bill to create a new system for handling non-secret information and to prevent the over-use of classification labels to keep information from the public. We hoped to change the DHS culture from "need to know"—the standard in the IC—to "need to share." In particular, the bill required that all DHS classified intelligence products be created in a standard unclassified format. Sensitive portions of the text could be marked classified and the remainder of the document could be widely shared. (Before, one sentence with secret information would render an entire multipage document classified.)

Our declassification bill was voted out of subcommittee unanimously in July 2008. After a tortuous journey through the House and Senate it was enacted in October 2010. I appreciated being invited to the Oval Office for President Obama's signing of the bill. To my surprise, I was the only one there as he signed the bill and gave me a ceremonial pen. The signature page, pen, and a picture of the event hung on the wall of my Wilson Center office, along with seven others from three administrations. Not too shabby to be author or principal co-author of eight laws!

DHS had been designated in 2003 as the lead federal agency for cybersecurity, then in its relative adolescence as a national security function of government. There was little debate about the growing scale of the cyberthreat, but the "war on turf" still needed to be fought. The U.S. military, through the National Security Agency (NSA) and later Cyber Command (CyberCom), was in charge of offensive and defensive cyber operations related to foreign governments. Defense agencies also helped protect the military's own enormous network infrastructure—all the ".mils." Nonetheless, the vast majority of all cybersystems are under the control of the private sector, including those for critical infrastructure such as electricity grids, the banking system, and water treatment plants. All of these private systems were supposed to fall under the purview of DHS, but the bulk of the technical capability was already resident in the Defense Department. Some objected to the notion of any military involvement in domestic cyber systems. But the alternative was to spend tens of billions of dollars re-creating NSA and CyberCom capabilities for DHS to police the domestic networks. Defense secretary Robert Gates and Homeland Security secretary Janet Napolitano bypassed their feuding staffs to produce a DoD-DHS memorandum of understanding. The concept was similar to that used when the military is called on for assistance during times of natural disasters such as hurricanes or wildfires, in which case a presidential order dispatches the military forces, which work under the control of FEMA. Under the new rules, the president would approve the use of the military's expertise in computer-network warfare, and DHS would direct the work. The goal was to ensure a rapid response to a cyberthreat while balancing concerns that civil liberties might be at risk should the military take over such domestic operations. It was an ad hoc arrangement that worked mostly because of the leaders involved, not because of any systematic legal framework or policy.

The administration's efforts were admirable, but Congress needed to step up. One of my last official acts as a member was to co-sponsor with Homeland Security chair Bennie

Thompson legislation to create a new Cybersecurity Compliance Division within DHS. Similar to the laws governing the chemical industry, DHS would share intelligence about cyberthreats against electric power plants with those plants' operators. In return, DHS would get better insight into the threat landscape and help improve security in facilities that needed it. The idea was to make the best possible use of existing structures and efforts, rather than implement wholesale bureaucratic changes. We submitted our legislation in November 2010 during the lame-duck session following the midterm elections. But once the Tea Party Republicans took over the House in 2011, our bill died.

Susan Collins would pick up the mantle in the Senate with the Cybersecurity Act of 2012, but she was unable to get a single vote from her Republican colleagues. Speaking later at a Wilson Center event, Susan would estimate that some 40 percent of the owners of core critical infrastructure— financial networks, water treatment plants, transportation systems—were still not hardening their computer systems sufficiently. She noted that some companies didn't even take such basic steps as changing the default password. For years they were essentially self-policing, wary of government involvement. A series of major hacks and denial-of-service attacks later showed that such a hands-off approach was unsustainable.

In the absence of congressional action, the Obama administration moved ahead to accomplish many of the cybersecurity objectives through executive order, though it would not have the same impact as legislation reflecting a bipartisan consensus of the Congress. Susan worried—and I agreed—that it provided a false sense of security that "something" was being done (the order would provide a framework for mostly voluntary action, but it could not ensure the needed liability protections provided by statute). DHS released a report at the end of 2012 reporting nearly 200 cyberattacks against the country's critical infrastructure over the prior year.

The problem was that DHS was set up originally to prevent another 9/11, not a "cyber Pearl Harbor." Businesses and other government agencies were not particularly responsive to DHS on cybersecurity because of its wobbly reputation, picked up early on—not just because of the FEMA response to Hurricane Katrina but also from a string of other black eyes, including the "underwear bomber" who, as late as December 2009, was able to board a flight and in the end was only stopped from blowing up the aircraft by alert airline passengers. The performance of DHS would improve greatly with the addition of Jeh Johnson as secretary in 2013 and, a year later, Suzanne Spaulding as undersecretary for the National Protection and Programs Directorate. I first got to know Spaulding as executive director of the Bremer Commission, a role in which she not only kept the various panelists on track but ended up writing most of the report. She became the Democratic staff director of HPSCI when I was ranking member.

But as lawmakers have found out, especially Susan Collins in 2012, an otherwise nonpolitical issue such as cybersecurity can become polarized when the public doesn't know the facts (or interest groups don't want to know the facts). One of my priorities at the Wilson Center was to bring together leaders from the NSA, Homeland Security, the FBI, civil liberties organizations, and other stakeholders to talk through these complex issues of privacy, technology, and security. The areas of overlap are surprisingly broad—at an October 2012 event it was interesting to see NSA director Keith Alexander and ACLU executive director Anthony Romero repeatedly agree with each other for about ten minutes before finally finding a point of contention.

Through trial and error, a reasonable government division of labor has developed with respect to cybersecurity in the domestic sphere: the NSA provides the most advanced technical tools and know-how, the FBI investigates breaches and other criminal violations, and DHS is responsible for public networks, collaboration with business, and protecting critical infrastructure (though the last of these is still overly dependent on voluntary compliance by the private sector). We recognized fairly early on that DHS would never be the leader in preventing cyberattacks. But it could help owners of critical infrastructure as they increasingly became targets for foreign adversaries looking to cause trouble just short of war.

Even as DHS accumulated more responsibilities in this area, the cybersecurity function remained buried a couple of layers down the bureaucracy (at assistant secretary level). In a rare example of recent bipartisanship, in November 2018 Congress passed (and President Trump signed) legislation bolstering its profile and clout through a new Cybersecurity and Infrastructure Security Agency (CISA) reporting directly to the DHS secretary. Suzanne Spaulding deserves major credit for laying the groundwork.

The United States is significantly better organized and prepared on cybersecurity than it was a decade ago. We've learned a great deal (the hard way) from the 2015 Chinese hack of tens of thousands of electronic files from the federal Office of Personnel Management (OPM), which led to major security upgrades (along with the resignation of top OPM executives). But our country has yet to be fully tested by a cyberattack with life-threatening consequences, as it surely will be. In December 2016, in the dead of winter, the Russians used a cyberattack on the Ukrainian electrical grid to turn off the lights in most of the country. Billions of so-called Internet of Things (IoT) devices, from smartphones to your refrigerator, are connecting to our networks. Many are made in China. Each is a point of vulnerability.

Congress, through oversight and some smart, narrowly tailored legislation—such as the newly created Senate-confirmed national cyber director in the 2021 National Defense Authorization Act—could play a positive role going forward. The new structure recently enacted at DHS has promise but needs to be fully empowered. Attacks in cyberspace are a real risk, though America has significant advantages over other nations—especially for early warning about potential threats. Technology services and telecommunications companies process most of the world's data which then transits

American-owned cables. Under FISA and other authorities, U.S. law enforcement can obtain information for national security purposes. Simply put: we own the pipes. Plus, advanced research is conducted by American universities and companies—or those of our allies in Europe and in Asia. It's vitally important to sustain that innovation ecosystem through sound investments, trade, and immigration policies. Let's not hand the other teams a win.

America is still reeling from the impact of COVID-19. Hundreds of thousands dead. Tens of millions unemployed. Public schools and universities shuttered. Early missteps have been widely reported, and corrective measures by the Biden administration are underway.

Congress is too often not a learning institution. Much of the time, in the absence of a crisis like 9/11 or Katrina that galvanizes the public, it struggles to take needed action, especially if the steps that should be taken are difficult or expensive. Experts have been warning about viral pandemics even longer than about cyberattacks. Preventing all outbreaks is impossible (nature, like the terrorists, only has to be lucky once), and once they've been ignited, pandemics require mitigation, recovery, and resilience. This is an entirely opposite dynamic from dealing with a terrorist-detonated nuclear weapon, in which prevention is everything because there is not much that can be done after the explosion. In 2006, the Pandemic and All-Hazards Preparedness Act, passed in the

wake of Hurricane Katrina, created a new division within
the Department of Health and Human Services (HHS). It
was assigned to manage the National Strategic Stockpile of
medical equipment such as gowns, masks, gurneys, and, as
would become the focus later, ventilators. The response to
the H1N1 swine flu pandemic in 2009 burned through much
of the stockpile, which was never fully replenished. In the
meantime, funding for the overall Public Health Emergency
Preparedness program declined in real terms by $300 mil-
lion from the mid-2000s—and, factoring in the inflation in
health care costs, the real decrease is much steeper.

While chairing my homeland security subcommittee, I
looked at the possibility of terrorists or rogue states creating
the same effect as a viral pandemic through bioengineering
or the release of toxins. In July 2008, Republican HPSCI
chair Mike Rogers and I first co-sponsored legislation that
updated the Select Agent Program. In the wake of the
post-911 anthrax attacks, this program regulated possession
and transfers of hazardous biological materials. Our bill expanded the category to cover a wider range of potentially
threatening toxins. "The threat of bioterrorism—whether a
smallpox outbreak, pandemic flu, or proliferation of deadly
ricin—is real," I said in a statement reintroducing the bill in
January 2009. "This isn't about playing the 'fear card,' this is
a call for a better action plan." Military labs storing germs
and other pathogens were well guarded and secure. I was
concerned in particular about the radiological material commonly found in unsecured hospital machines that could be
repurposed into a weapon.

At a September 2009 hearing I asked HHS secretary Kathleen Sebelius if the set of protocols in place for the ongoing H1N1 virus pandemic was applicable to a possible biological attack. Her response was that when it came to developing vaccines, informing the public, distributing health supplies, and interactions with state and local government, it would be very similar. The challenge, she said, was "we just haven't done it nationally nearly in forty years." In January 2010, the independent Commission on Weapons of Mass Destruction Proliferation and Terrorism, which produced a comprehensive "World at Risk" report at the end of the Bush 43 administration, gave the United States government a grade of "F" for bioterrorism preparedness in a follow-up assessment. Led by former Senate Intelligence Committee chair Bob Graham and former Republican senator Jim Talent, the commission concluded that the response to the H1N1 outbreak did not bode well for our preparedness for bioterrorism. The swine flu epidemic peaked after several months, by which time most Americans had access to the vaccine. But as the report said, "a bio-attack will come with no such warning." The commission had earlier warned that a bioterror attack was more likely than an attack with a nuclear or chemical device because it is easier and cheaper to pull off for groups without access to state backing or scientific expertise.

Unlike in cyberattacks, domestic terrorism, and natural disasters, Homeland Security would play a supporting role to HHS in the event of a pandemic, human-made or otherwise. An office within DHS would provide models, updated annually, showing the impact on the country's critical infrastructure as a result of a significant part of its workforce becoming sick (e.g., how an outbreak among Federal Aviation Administration employees would affect air traffic control). The computer-assisted models consistently showed shortages of personal protective equipment, vaccines, and other supplies. According to *Politico*, those computer-assisted models were released every year from 2005 to 2017 and then stopped due to a bureaucratic dispute within the Trump administration. The Pandemic and All Hazards Preparedness Act was reauthorized in 2018 with some constructive reforms, but the necessary funding and top-level attention never followed.

In many respects the biggest underlying challenge to DHS, which impacts everything, is the "original sin" of setting up the department without a rational congressional oversight structure. Congress has been unable to assert a single, principal point of oversight and review for homeland security issues (akin to the role of the armed services committees with respect to the Defense Department). Eighty-eight committees and subcommittees have some piece of the homeland security mission, and at times the department leadership feels like it has testified before every one of them. I recall a chart modeled after the *Where's Waldo?* images that shows the crazy number of committees and subcommittees with some oversight participating in the conference session to reauthorize DHS; one would see no fewer than 80 people sitting around the table representing the different committees with jurisdiction over some part of the department.

No powerful committee chair wanted to give up jurisdiction of a high-visibility function—whether Treasury over
the Secret Service, Justice over the Border Patrol, or Transportation over the Coast Guard. In the Senate, Susan Collins
and Joe Lieberman on the Homeland Security and Government Affairs Committee overcame some of these structural
flaws during the decade following 9/11. But the Homeland
Security Committee in the House has too little jurisdiction,
which contributes to management difficulties within DHS.
There, decisions are still largely stovepiped along the lines of
the original twenty-two agencies. Department leaders have
spoken of going to one House subcommittee to get one set
of instructions and then receiving completely opposite di-
rections from another subcommittee that owns a part of the
DHS function. It is past time to streamline the committee
structure overseeing DHS as a necessary step toward stream-
lining the organization of the department.

The attacks of 9/11 provided a wake-up call letting us
know that our government was not properly organized to
secure the homeland given the new realities of the twenty-
first century. DHS has since achieved many of the goals set
by its original creators, above all the absence of a catastrophic
mass-casualty attack; back on September 12, 2001, none of
us would have predicted that we would have gone so long
without another one. We have also been forced to muddle
through with a Rube Goldberg–style congressional oversight apparatus, high leadership vacancy rates within the
department, and an overreliance on private contractors. It
is not clear how the COVID-19 crisis will play out, but we

have learned enough already to know that changes are urgent to the way our government prepares for the next assault
on the homeland, whether it comes via explosives, cyberattack, or viruses. Looming dangers to the homeland are
real—the question is whether U.S. political institutions and
the public are ready.

THREE

Power over Truth
Corrupts Intelligence

I have fond memories of my late husband, Sidney Harman. This one goes back to the fall of 2002. It had been a little over a year since the shocking September 11 attacks. Coming home after another long day of intelligence briefings, meetings, and hearings on Capitol Hill, I told Sidney I'd made a decision: "I'm going to vote for the Iraq War." Sidney didn't respond at first. After twenty-two years of marriage, he didn't need to. He just shot me The Look. Anyone in a relationship knows what that is—an all-knowing arch of an eyebrow, a pursing of the lips, a slight tilt of the head. This expression has exasperated spouses since the beginning of time. I explained (again) my reasons: that Saddam Hussein had thwarted UN inspections and sanctions for more than a decade while stockpiling chemical and biological weapons for use against the United States and our allies.

"Janie, that's a lot of crap," said Sidney.

"How do you know that?" I sputtered. "You haven't read what I've read or seen what I've seen in my travels to different intelligence services. You may be a brilliant businessman, but you don't know the intel world."

He shrugged. "You'll see."

As it turned out, the U.S. intelligence community was operating under a 1947 business model in the lead-up to 9/11, and then it botched the prewar assessments of Iraq. Intelligence was reformed in important ways afterward but remains vulnerable to manipulation by the White House. We still confront digital-age intelligence challenges using industrial-age organizations subject to political interference. This insanity will continue unless we give the director of national intelligence real power to do the job, reduce over-classification, and reform archaic hiring and security clearance practices that keep the IC from getting people with the most critical language skills and cultural knowledge.

Intelligence is not policy. It's not science either. Intelligence is a set of predictions based on the best facts about human intentions and adversary capability. Despite warnings given by the CIA about Al Qaeda, the U.S. government was blindsided by the 9/11 attacks, which were unprecedented in scale, sophistication, and ruthlessness. Additionally, if intelligence is distorted, cherry-picked, or slanted to fit what the policymaker wants to hear, it will inevitably lead to poor outcomes. Good intelligence doesn't guarantee good policy, but bad intelligence will almost certainly lead to bad policy. Iraq would turn out to be a toxic combination of both. These two systematic intelligence failures called out for a major reform of the U.S. intelligence community.

We are unlikely again to see failures similar to 9/11 and

Iraq: dots unconnected, bogus assumptions unchallenged. But making certain the IC stays true to its mission to speak truth to power requires constant vigilance. The good news is that agencies that make up the IC align priorities and share information in ways unheard of two decades go. The analytical products are rigorous and vetted for alternative views. The career intelligence workforce is as professional, talented, and dedicated as ever. The CIA has become remarkably effective in its covert and paramilitary role—surveilling, capturing, interrogating, or killing the most dangerous terrorists. Yet these tactical successes have not translated into overall victory against violent extremist groups, which requires defeating first their appeal and ideology. It is not helpful that under President Trump the motivations and loyalty of the IC came under assault from the White House and its congressional allies. Top-level career officers resigned or were removed. The Office of the Director of National Intelligence (ODNI) was politicized, and the rank and file were undermined. Fortunately, the new Biden team understands that the nature of the threats America faces keeps evolving—as does the kind of intelligence capabilities we need.

When I arrived in the Congress in 1993, the Soviet Union had recently disintegrated. As we transitioned away from the Cold War, it was a fascinating and challenging time to oversee American intelligence. My Southern California congressional district produced many of the sophisticated space products used by the IC for surveillance and collection, but—as discussed earlier—intelligence and defense budgets were coming down fast, and my constituents were getting hammered. So I sought a seat on the House Permanent Select Committee on Intelligence, but did not succeed in getting one at that point. Nonetheless, my service on the House Armed Services Committee during the 1990s still provided a window into the workings of the U.S. intelligence enterprise. Most of the overall intelligence spending went through the Defense Department to fund the National Security Agency, the Defense Intelligence Agency, the National Reconnaissance Office, and the National Geospatial-Intelligence Agency (NGA). Joining HPSCI in 1997, I became fully read in to the IC's capabilities and culture, led then by the CIA. I visited a number of agencies, met with both the leadership and the rank and file, and learned to interpret highly classified material generally not available to members of the HASC (though it took me a while to learn "intel-speak"— the acronyms used routinely by briefers and analysts).

The Bremer Commission on Terrorism recommended improvements in collection, surveillance, and dissemination. At the time, the biggest point of contention was the 1995 guideline imposed by CIA director John Deutsch requiring top management approval to recruit foreign agents. Because of earlier scandals, the Agency's management shied from working with assets who had less than pristine backgrounds. The problem, of course, is that when it comes to terror groups, it is impossible to get anyone on the inside who does not have some blood on their hands. This was not a totally novel dilemma. The FBI had been paying and cutting immunity deals with the worst-of-the-worst Mafia henchmen for decades. The commission settled on retaining the higher-approval requirement for recruiting at the CIA but put in place legal safeguards that permitted officers to be more aggressive. As I would explain to the Senate Intelligence Committee after the report's release: "I didn't want to let the new agent in the field have sole responsibility for the decision, both because he might make the wrong decision or because, even if he made the right decision, he would then become a political target later if for some reason it didn't turn out well." The CIA would claim after 9/11 that the Deutsch guidelines never stopped them from recruiting an important foreign source.

After the 9/11 attacks I fought off the knee-jerk reaction in much of Congress and the news media to blame the CIA. During my time on the Bremer Commission and HPSCI, I had come to know and admire many intelligence officers, from those in foreign stations all the way to the top brass in Langley. They were already demoralized, many filled with personal guilt, by the failure to stop the attacks and by the harsh criticisms that followed. More so than any other agency of government, the CIA would need to be at its best in the fight against Al Qaeda. On the Hill and in media appearances I made a point of defending the CIA. It was under George Tenet's leadership that the Agency stepped out of its post–Cold War haze to focus on global terrorism. There were, in fact, several important successes during the later 1990s, including foiling the Millennium Plot targeting Los Angeles and other locations at the end of 1999. Whatever its shortcomings, the CIA was the only part of the federal government to have taken Al Qaeda seriously, and its analysts had issued multiple warnings to that effect. Overall, the FBI had much more to answer for, as did the White House. Ultimately, I saw 9/11 as more of a failure of government coordination and policy than an intelligence failure.

George Tenet in particular was in the crosshairs of congressional Republicans. It was convenient to focus blame on the Democratic holdover from the Clinton administration rather than on the surprisingly incurious new Republican president. In the wake of 9/11, I thought it would be a mistake to fire Tenet, who knew more about Al Qaeda than anyone likely to take his place. A former staff director for the Senate intelligence committee, Tenet was the rare director of central intelligence—DCI, as the CIA position was then called—who cultivated Capitol Hill. Tenet was also excellent at forging relationships with foreign intelligence agencies—typically over wine and cigars with their leaders—that would prove to be useful later. By and large the DCI position attracts more-reserved personalities, but Tenet was a charismatic and garrulous character who walked the halls of the Agency late at night chatting with anyone he encountered, regardless of rank. In January 2002, during a HPSCI trip to the Middle East, I was struck by how many CIA officers in the stations we visited credited Tenet with lifting morale after the attacks.

Keeping Tenet at the CIA to lead the first counterattack against Al Qaeda may have been prudent, but it exacted a cost later. He was indebted to President Bush for keeping him in a plum position coveted by any number of influential

Republicans. Bush also defended him publicly after 9/11. So when some in the White House later began to distort and inflate CIA findings to justify a new war in Iraq, Tenet was in less of a position to push back.

The congressional joint inquiry on 9/11 concluded its work in December 2002. In a statement accompanying the report I wrote: "To date, the term 'Intelligence Community' has been an oxymoron. The community is really a collection of stovepipes working separately—often in conflicting or self-interested ways." I endorsed one of the report's principal recommendations: the creation of the position of director of national intelligence (DNI). The DNI would bring cohesion in priorities and budgeting to the different collection and analysis agencies, regardless of which cabinet department they belonged to. At the time—late 2002 and early 2003—congressional focus had turned almost entirely to Iraq, and intelligence reform was pushed to the back burner.

The story of the CIA and Iraq's WMD has been told many times. Nearly twenty years later, it is still staggering—and anguishing—to think how so many smart, well-intentioned, and knowledgeable people could have gotten so much so wrong. The intelligence failures leading to the Iraq War had roots in intelligence shortcomings before the Gulf War. Iraq's invasion of Kuwait in 1990 came as a big surprise to the CIA—and everyone else. At the end of Operation Desert Storm, the CIA would discover that Iraq's nuclear weapons program was much further along than had been thought. Saddam was already known to have used chemical weapons against Iranian soldiers and Kurdish civilians, to devastating effect. But the extent of Iraqi progress by 1991 to develop a nuclear weapon was jarring to top leaders in the Bush 41 administration, including defense secretary Dick Cheney and his undersecretary, Paul Wolfowitz. Both men had tangled with the CIA many years earlier over estimates of Soviet military strength, and both would be highly influential in pushing the most alarmist view of Iraq.

In the lead-up to the 2003 invasion, the Office of Special Plans was set up in the Pentagon to funnel reports to the White House about supposed connections between Iraq and Al Qaeda. The specter of nuclear attack was invoked, with national security advisor Condoleezza Rice saying, "We don't want the smoking gun to be a mushroom cloud." I felt a special responsibility to be thorough and accurate, given my position as a HPSCI member and my reputation for bipartisanship on national security. The October 2002 NIE on Iraq was impressive—or seemed to be. So too was Colin Powell's presentation to the United Nations in January 2003, which, we learned later, was based on dubious material provided by the Pentagon and White House.

The regime was toppled in a brilliant display of U.S. military prowess. But by the summer of 2003 it was clear something had gone seriously awry in the prewar intelligence assessment. Nonetheless, the CIA leadership and White House continued to stick firmly—though increasingly nervously—to their Iraq WMD talking points. By then I was the ranking member on HPSCI.

After visiting Iraq as part of a four-person delegation led by the committee's chair, Porter Goss, I opened up our next committee hearing in mid-July with a summary of what we had learned in recent weeks about prewar intelligence. The case for war relied far more on "circumstantial indicators" of Iraq WMD programs than solid facts. The information presented to Congress by the administration did not reflect the many "gaps and uncertainties" in the raw intelligence. In particular, the claim that Saddam Hussein tried to buy uranium yellowcake from Niger should never have made it into the 2003 State of the Union message. Iraq's "denial and deception" efforts were less about concealing the nonexistent WMD and more about preserving the regime's survival. The intelligence community "did not adequately warn about the prospects for looting" after the collapse of the regime, which also hampered the subsequent search for WMD.

Reflecting the seriousness of the situation—and the bipartisanship that still existed on the HPSCI—Goss and I sent a joint letter to Tenet in September describing "significant deficiencies" in the CIA's ability to account for Iraq's behavior after UN inspectors departed in 1998. The significance of Goss's participation in the letter was not lost on anyone: he was seen as supportive of the White House and close personally to the CIA, where he had started his career as an intelligence officer. If Goss would go on record with criticisms, then things had to be bad.

In response, national security advisor Condoleezza Rice asserted that "nothing pointed to a reversal of Saddam Hussein's very active efforts to acquire weapons of mass destruction." This was the White House line. I expected the CIA line might be different. After six months of fruitless searching for WMD in Iraq after the toppling of Saddam's regime, the CIA spokesman said that the Agency "stands fully behind its findings and judgements." But by January 2004, David Kay, a former UN weapons inspector appointed by the administration to investigate the absence of WMD in Iraq, concluded, "It turns out that we were all wrong." The response by Tenet was to give a speech in February at Georgetown University (his alma mater). He rejected Kay's conclusions and asserted the jury was still out on the Iraq NIE. He stuck with the prewar allegation, by then mostly discredited, that Iraqi aluminum tubes were being used to develop nuclear weapons. That no biological weapons had been discovered was less important than Iraq's intentions to pursue them, which the CIA continued to assert. By taking this line, Tenet did himself and his agency no favors, making it harder and harder for his defenders, including me, to argue he was still the right person for the job.

In Iraq, the basic underlying assumptions about the regime—not just on WMD but its overall capabilities and intentions with respect to terrorism and regional domination—turned out to be completely wrong. (To its credit, the State Department's in-house intelligence bureau voiced doubts not reflected in the published NIE and was most prescient about the chaos that would follow a U.S. invasion.) The U.S. intel-

ligence community's stumbles on Iraq's WMD would force
us to question what else was being missed about the rest of
the Axis of Evil (Iran and North Korea). And they spelled the
end of the doctrine of preemption less than a year after it had
been announced. The United States would not start a major
war—much less invade a sovereign country—based on what
intelligence estimates said a foreign actor might possess or
might do in the future. The combined sins of omission and
commission, revealed by 9/11 and Iraq, respectively, demonstrated the need for a dramatically new approach to national
intelligence, and for a new governing structure to manage it.

As with homeland security, the momentum toward reform of
national intelligence functions built slowly. After the collapse
of the Soviet Union there was a push for intelligence reform
during the Bush 41 administration; however, that effort ran
into resistance from Dick Cheney, who was then defense secretary, and CIA director Robert Gates—resistance that was
a foretaste of the battle lines that would be drawn more than
a decade later. The sticking point was the assertion that creating the post of an overall national intelligence chief would
mean a downgrading of the role of the CIA director, who
presided over a small community management service. This
was more a blow to prestige than to substance, as in fact the
CIA director did very little management of other IC elements. George Tenet's "declaration of war" on Al Qaeda in
1998, for example, had minimal impact outside the CIA. Additionally, most of the nation's intelligence budget—some 80

percent—was buried in Pentagon accounts, and no secretary of defense would give up those assets without a fight. The federal intelligence apparatus—designed after World War II to prevent another Pearl Harbor and optimized to compete with the Soviet Union—had been retained, with only minor tinkering, after the end of the Cold War. As I've stressed several times already, we entered the twenty-first century with a 1947 business model.

Once the Iraq miss became evident, a determined group of bipartisan reformers on the Hill—"adventurous souls," as I called us—took on the task of crafting legislation to reform the IC. Skeptics pointed out, accurately, that a centralized organization would not fix the groupthink that had led to the flawed Iraq intelligence estimates and their use to justify a war. Any serious reform would also have to overhaul the conduct of analysis to ensure that so-called red-teaming—establishing a group to make arguments against the prevailing consensus—was built into the process. In March 2004 I told the Council on Foreign Relations: "Never assume that one hypothesis is the only hypothesis. Test everything. And when the analytic products are written, do a better job than we did in that 2002 NIE. Put on the front page for dummies like me not only what we think we know, but what we don't know." I quoted former CIA director Robert Gates, himself a career agency analyst, who had written years earlier that analysts should highlight what they *don't know* and resist the temptation to go beyond that under the guise of "making the tough calls." But in the run-up to the invasion of Iraq, analysts spoke precisely of "making the tough calls" and, worse, "making the case" for war. Some analysts who'd worked on the October 2002 NIE told me they believed a decision to go to war had already been made months earlier.

Here too, I tried to follow the model of Senator Henry "Scoop" Jackson, the hawkish Cold War Democrat, who once said, "In matters of national security, the best politics is no politics." I was still trying to keep the focus on what Republicans and Democrats in the Congress working with the White House could do to fix the problems. In that spirit I decided in March 2004 to give a speech on intelligence reform to the American Enterprise Institute (AEI), a right-of-center think tank. The AEI speech provided an opportunity to give President Bush credit where it was due on Afghanistan— then still considered a success—but also to present some hard truths about the intelligence on Iraq in the lead-up to the war.

Prior to my speech, the White House, growing increasingly defensive politically on anything related to Iraq, agreed to another outside commission. This one would be led by former Democratic senator Chuck Robb and former Republican deputy attorney general and D.C. circuit court judge Laurence Silberman. The commission's mandate was to examine how faulty intelligence had been generated—but not how that intelligence had been used or misused by policymakers. And the Robb-Silberman Commission would not report back until *after* the 2004 election. I found the delay problematic, because I knew the world would not stand still for another year. Neither would the terrorists. So in my AEI speech I compared the White House posture to an auto mechanic who says, "I'm sorry I can't fix your brakes this week, but don't worry because I made your horn louder."

As it turned out, further investigation soon confirmed some of our initial fears about prewar Iraq intelligence. Saddam's alleged scheme to get uranium yellowcake from Niger—mentioned in the 2003 State of the Union address—was a total crock. So too were the allegations of Iraqi bioweapons labs that had been made by an Iraqi exile in Germany who was code-named Curveball. This source was distrusted by German intelligence—which told the United States as much—and had never been interviewed by the CIA. Particularly galling to me was the finding that claims that Iraq had been building uncrewed aerial vehicles to spray chemical weapons in the United States were also bogus, because those allegations had factored into my decision to vote for the war.

On April 1, 2004, several Democratic HPSCI members and I introduced legislation to create the post of director of national intelligence, outside (and above) the CIA. Unlike the DHS secretary, who was explicitly in charge of all the agencies collected into the department, this leader would not "own" the IC agencies directly. Rather, the DNI would function like a military joint commander, with significant budgetary control, the ability to task satellites operated by the Defense Department for national strategic priorities, and the power to create IC-wide "mission centers" with different areas of focus.

In early June, Bush announced Tenet's resignation on the

South Lawn of the White House as he was preparing to de-
part for Andrews Air Force Base. By the time the president
was airborne I issued a statement that my staff later called
"Tenet Out, DNI In," reflecting our view that a major
roadblock had been removed to achieving real intelligence
reform.

A more powerful impetus for change was the 9/11 Commission. It was created in late November 2002—over initial
objections by the White House—to take a broad and systematic look at the failure to prevent the 9/11 attacks, from
shortcomings in intelligence to law enforcement to air traffic control. The commissioners were led by Tom Kean, who
had been a popular Republican governor of New Jersey, and
my Wilson Center predecessor, former Indiana Democratic
congressman Lee Hamilton. The 9/11 Commission's hearings during the summer of 2004 drew national attention.
In one televised session, John Lehman, Ronald Reagan's
navy secretary, spoke about what he called the CIA culture of "smugness and even arrogance." Looking at Tenet,
who was sitting at the witness table, Lehman said: "There's
a train coming down the track, there are going to be very
real changes made. You've done a terrific job in evolution-
ary change, but it's clearly not been enough. Revolution is
coming."

The commission's final report, released in July 2004 to
great fanfare, included recommendations for intelligence reorganization similar to those in the legislation I had introduced three months earlier. The White House and other
opponents were now playing defense. I issued a statement

saying, "It is time for the President to snap out of his deep state of denial about intelligence failures." The stars all seemed aligned for a major reform bill before the 2004 election.

But a major rearguard action was under way. Defense secretary Donald Rumsfeld adamantly opposed any reform that would loosen the Pentagon's control over the military intelligence-support agencies. He had a strong congressional ally in HASC chair Duncan Hunter, who considered migrating any authority outside the Pentagon a dangerous abrogation of the military chain of command. Colin Powell, the secretary of state and a former chair of the Joint Chiefs of Staff, had testified that more centralization would improve the quality of military intelligence, but Hunter remained unconvinced. As with homeland security, winning the war on terror in the intelligence arena also required winning the "war on turf."

With Hunter's encouragement and Rumsfeld's acquiescence, and without the knowledge of the White House, Joint Chiefs of Staff chair General Richard Myers released a letter insisting that the Pentagon continue to control funding for the alphabet soup of mostly technical collection agencies supporting the military. As it turned out, however, the three-star officers leading the NSA and NGA were strong advocates for reform—even going as far as to recommend the creation of a Department of Intelligence. At one point they met with senior White House officials "off the calendar" so Rumsfeld wouldn't find out. NGA director James Clapper, an Air Force lieutenant general, became persona non grata at the Pentagon because he testified in favor of reform.

Ultimately, what helped the legislation move along was the decision by Senate majority leader Bill Frist to turn management of the bill over to the Senate Government Affairs and Homeland Security Committee, led by Maine Republican Susan Collins and Connecticut Democrat Joe Lieberman. Each was a centrist—Lieberman a hawkish Democrat, Collins one of the last of the New England Republicans. They forged the compromises that would create a passable bill. These included refinements in language regarding the military chain of command, to satisfy Duncan Hunter. House Intelligence Committee chair Pete Hoekstra and I worked very closely with Collins and Lieberman—collectively we were known as the "Big Four" during this process—and it was during those intense after-hours deliberations that my close friendship with Collins really deepened. ("Susan Collins rocks!" I proclaimed in the conference committee in which the House and Senate versions of the bill were being debated and reconciled.) Alongside the many weighty matters discussed, we also considered an appropriate title for this new intelligence chief. One of the first suggestions was "national intelligence director." I pointed out that the acronym would be "NID," which sounded more like a bug. Or, worse, like "nit"—as in "nitpicker," which intelligence people were often accused of being. That idea was dropped, and the title "director of national intelligence" was selected.

Susan and Joe certainly did their part in the Senate. After some 300 amendments, the comprehensive bill passed on the

Senate floor by a vote of 96 to 2. And even though Hoekstra and I largely agreed with the Senate approach, we knew it was not going to be that easy in the House. Hunter and Representative Jim Sensenbrenner, chair of the Judiciary Committee, continued to dig in their heels, and they carried with them much of the Republican conference. The negotiations involving factions of the Congress, the Pentagon, and White House would continue into the fall, with House conservatives refusing to budge. (Under the informal principle known as the "Hastert Rule," the Speaker would not advance a bill that did not have the support of a majority of Republicans, even if it would otherwise pass easily with only Democratic votes.) It became clear that despite the support of the president (and Senator John Kerry, his Democratic challenger), there would be no resolution before the 2004 election.

By the December lame-duck session, the clock was ticking. A new Congress would require starting almost from scratch in January. Ultimately, the parties agreed that the bill shall "respect and not abrogate" the authority of the cabinet agencies—meaning the Department of Defense. The result was that the DNI would provide guidance on budgetary and personnel matters to the intelligence community, but the military chain of command would remain unaltered.

The final product was a less ambitious version of the legislation I had first proposed in April, and well short of what the Kean-Hamilton Commission recommended. I would have preferred to see the DNI serve a ten-year term, like the FBI director, thus insulating the position as much as possible from partisan influences. Still, the Intelligence Reform and Terrorism Prevention Act (IRTPA), signed on December 17, 2004, was a major achievement. Though the debate over structure and authorities generated the most attention, the bill contained significant changes to practices and policies as well. It prescribed a more vigorous analysis process (which had been the major failing with the Iraq intelligence), created the National Counter-Terrorism Center to connect foreign and domestic intelligence (the major failing leading up to 9/11), and established a civil liberties board to ensure that safeguards were baked into the front end of policymaking.

To be sure, IRTPA did not inoculate the intelligence community against future mistakes, missed cues, or bad leaders. Also, some reform provisions were implemented better than others (for example, the civil liberties board was left vacant by Bush and Obama for nearly a decade). But the major changes have mostly stood the test of time, though the need for continuous reevaluation and reform of the IC never stops.

The first DNI, John Negroponte, immediately got off the wrong foot by retaining the title "ambassador." If anyone deserved that honorific, it was John—over nearly four decades of impressive diplomatic service he'd been ambassador five times, including to the United Nations and to Iraq. But he was now leading the U.S. intelligence community, not working at the State Department. I also worried that Negroponte conceded too much to the Pentagon on satellite programs, which was one of the major authorities given to the DNI. After almost two years, he resigned as DNI and became deputy secretary of state, a post he sought out. Technically it was a step down in rank, but far more in his comfort zone.

The 2006 midterms ushered in a Democratic majority in both houses of Congress. They also brought about personnel changes with significant implications for the IC. Don Rumsfeld, long a CIA antagonist, was out at the Pentagon (as was his intelligence chief, Steve Cambone, whose relationship with the Agency had long since turned toxic). I too was out at HPSCI, which will be discussed in Chapter 7. But I would continue to engage the IC and track its performance from my perch as chair of the Homeland Security Subcommittee on Intelligence, Information Sharing, and Terrorism Risk Assessment.

The DNI position would be filled by a succession of retired military officers: first Mike McConnell, for the balance of the Bush presidency; then, for a short period under Obama, retired four-star admiral Dennis Blair; following him, James Clapper (after serving as undersecretary of defense for intelligence for Gates). The law required the DNI to have significant national security and intelligence experience. Some people worried about the "militarization" of U.S. intelligence; in 2006 HPSCI chair Pete Hoekstra had even voted against Air Force general Mike Hayden, the nominee of Bush 43 to be CIA director, believing it set the wrong precedent to have a military officer in that post. I was less concerned with the uniform they wore or used to wear. The precursor to the CIA, the Office of Strategic Services, was a paramilitary organization led by a major general (the legendary Bill Donovan). Several career military men had previously served as CIA director, though none since Admiral Stansfield Turner's rocky tenure in the Carter administration. What really mattered was their effectiveness guiding the sixteen agencies of the IC, their relationship with (and respect for) the Congress, and independence, to the extent possible, from White House manipulation or politics.

The limitations of the DNI's authority—and the importance of political savvy—were laid bare during Blair's short tenure under President Obama. Unlike the other retired generals and admirals taking IC leadership posts, Blair was not a military intelligence officer. He was a surface fleet officer whose last assignment had been leading all U.S. forces in the Pacific, from Pearl Harbor to South Korea.

Then came the surprising decision by Obama to make Leon Panetta his CIA director. Leon may not have had an intelligence background, but he was one of the most experienced and effective operators in D.C. He had chaired the House Budget Committee, been director of OMB, and later served as chief of staff under President Clinton. He knew how the White House worked and how to talk to a president. Blair early on tried to mark his DNI territory by claiming the authority to name the U.S. intelligence chief of station in foreign countries, to include potentially putting non-CIA people in the post. For sixty years that position had been the exclusive province of the CIA. Panetta was having none of it, and he got the president's support. Blair would be gone as DNI after a little more than a year in the job.

After becoming the fourth DNI in the five years since the position was created, Jim Clapper would serve from August 2010 until the end of the Obama administration, providing the steadiness and continuity needed for the organization to settle into its proper role. (Full disclosure: When I left Congress, Clapper surprised me by offering me the National Intelligence Distinguished Public Service Medal at my farewell party. I then served on the DNI Senior Advisory Group at his request.) Clapper came closest to what Colin Powell, in advocating for the establishment of the position, called "an empowered quarterback"—coordinating the various IC agencies but not trying to run them or pick fights with their leaders, and having the ear of the president but not being captive to the White House. In Clapper's case, fifty years of government service—in the military and in the Defense Department—had produced long-standing relationships and influence that could not always be replicated. When CIA director Panetta replaced Gates as defense secretary in 2011 and U.S. Army general David Petraeus took over the CIA soon after, the solid relationships between them and DNI Clapper suggested that the synergy and harmony that had developed between defense and intelligence would continue.

One of the unsung accomplishments—indeed, transformations—of the post-9/11 era was the effective fusion of intelligence assets, both technical and personnel, with the U.S. military special operations forces. These include the famed Navy SEALs, the U.S. Army's Delta Force and Rangers, the Marine Raiders, and highly trained U.S. Air Force pilots and their specialized aircraft. These missions would lead to the killing or capture of most of Al Qaeda's leadership in Iraq—recognized later as a key factor in the military success of the 2007 surge—and, most famously, the takedown of Osama Bin Laden in 2011.

Institutionally, there were undeniable advances resulting from the reform legislation: the reconciling of different information-technology systems, the centrally coordinated tasking of satellites in keeping with national priorities, uniform audit standards, a more careful acquisitions system, and a more vigorous process to assemble and "red-team" intelligence estimates. Borrowing from the Goldwater-Nichols Department of Defense Reorganization Act of 1986, which required officers to complete a joint duty assignment to be eligible for promotion to the top ranks, the reforms gave midlevel agents the opportunity to broaden their experience by working outside their home agencies.

The IC's record of predicting major events remained spotty, however. The U.S. government was blindsided by the Arab Spring, the war in Syria, the rise of ISIS, and Russia's seizure of Crimea. In April 2011, the United States joined another military campaign for regime change in Libya. This intervention through NATO was justified to the American public and the UN Security Council by predictions, later deemed exaggerated, of an impending massacre of hundreds of thousands of people in Benghazi. The planned attacks by militants on U.S. diplomats there on the anniversary of 9/11 were attributed by administration leaders—most famously UN ambassador Susan Rice on a round of Sunday interview shows—to an anti-Islamic video produced in California.

Unlike in Iraq, the Libya miscalculations were not followed by a large and costly U.S. military occupation. But they highlighted the continued need to be vigilant when it came to the use of intelligence estimates to support policy objectives. By the time of the Arab Spring and Libya I would be at the Wilson Center, but I continued to keep close ties in the IC and monitor, with some sense of ownership, the performance of the DNI and the outcome of the legislation I had helped pull over the finish line years earlier.

At the start there was enormous skepticism about the DNI position and office, especially within the CIA, which had lost its singular role as the leader of the community. Leaders I respected, including John McLaughlin, who was serving as acting CIA director when the reform passed, initially opposed the concept. But he and others would conclude that under Clapper the position came into its own after 2010. The ODNI would take on many "housekeeping" functions for the other intelligence agencies, including shaping budgets, providing the President's Daily Brief, running legislative affairs, and, most famously under President Trump, overseeing whistleblowing and source protection. The DNI would be the president's principal advisor, but the CIA director would get plenty of access to the president.

Nonetheless, by the end of the Obama administration I was concerned that the ODNI was growing into something it was not intended to be—a mini cabinet agency. We had designed it to be a lean, nimble command focused on coordinating the activities of agencies, not on replicating them. The ODNI was supposed to rise above the intelligence bureaucracy, not be part of it with top-heavy directorates for major functions. When John Negroponte arrived in 2005 he had eleven support staff—far too few, to be sure. By 2008 ODNI's workforce had grown to 1,750. Along with the National Security Council (NSC), it would grow even larger under Obama. Other community members, the CIA in particular, had legitimate gripes about the DNI's dense concentration of senior executive service positions—scarce and coveted positions in the civil service. In February 2017, after Trump took office, Pete Hoekstra and I wrote in the *Wall Street Journal* that the transition presented an opportunity to slim down a DNI operation that had become, as the headline said, "bloated and overly complex." From our perspective, "the more ODNI grows, the less quickly it can move." We noted that it had taken the private cybersecurity firm CrowdStrike a month to investigate the digital break-in at the Democratic National Committee during the 2016 presidential campaign and publish a detailed report attributing the hack to Russia. But it took the IC far longer to consolidate around the same assessment. Rumored disagreements between the CIA and FBI leaked into the press, which, as we pointed out, "fed the fog of Russian disinformation." Nimble or agile this was not. Reprising concerns that went back to the Bush administration, we wrote that "the problem is exacerbated by ODNI's increasingly public image. The director was never meant to be a chief spokesman on intelligence issues, but one after another has found himself playing that role. Spies need to 'go dark.'"

It was reassuring to see former senator Dan Coats get the

nod as DNI in March 2017. Unlike his immediate predecessors, Coats was not a career military intelligence professional, but he had served on the Senate Intelligence Committee and in one of America's top diplomatic posts as ambassador to Germany. I told CNN that, given his distinguished political and diplomatic career, "this is a job he didn't need." But, speaking "as one of the great-grandparents of the director of National Intelligence position," I said that "he fits the bill." Nonetheless, Coats was quickly marginalized; he was surprised to learn—at a public forum, no less—that the president had praised Vladimir Putin and discounted the IC's assessment that Russia interfered with the 2016 election. He eventually resigned. Richard Grenell was installed as acting DNI while also serving as ambassador to Germany, and he led a purge of senior people deemed insufficiently loyal to the White House. After nearly a year without a Senate-confirmed DNI, a relatively junior congressman, Texas Republican John Ratcliff, was confirmed in late May 2020 on a near party-line vote.

Our bipartisan efforts to stand up a professional, apolitical DNI were unraveling. As I wrote in the *New York Times*, "It's a really bad day at the office when the spooks are spooked." Invoking the machinations of Porter Goss's top political aides against the career experts at CIA fifteen years earlier, I wrote, "we've seen this movie before, and it didn't end well." A purge of our best and brightest intelligence officers will have a highly negative effect on long-standing relationships with our allies' intelligence services: they will no longer trust sensitive information from the United States if our own agents and analysts are pressured to skew results for political reasons.

And, as I wrote, "it's impossible to know how many clues we will miss if our intelligence community is isolated from the world and the president's daily brief only reinforces what the Administration wants to hear."

The American intelligence enterprise is much improved since establishing the ODNI structure in 2004, but it is still struggling to respond to a chaotic digital age. New ideas for restructuring come and go. Obama's last CIA director, John Brennan, proposed dividing the Agency into ten "mission centers," each combining operations and analysis. As I wrote in *Foreign Affairs* in early 2015, "rearranging the deck chairs will not be enough to prepare the intelligence community for the challenges that lie ahead. Instead, Washington must venture beyond the conventional wisdom and reckon with an alternative vision of the future." Some traditionalists, including Brennan, were concerned that the CIA had become too paramilitary. But there is no avoiding the reality that the Agency's leading mission will continue to be covert action, reflecting its OSS roots and post-9/11 expertise. Covert drone strikes have become a source of friction in America's relationship with the Muslim world, but if used correctly and with restraint, they can remain a valuable part of the CIA's tool kit.

While human intelligence, or "humint," remains valuable and the central function of the CIA, the world has changed dramatically since the time when the principal job of a CIA agent was to use embassy cover to recruit diplomats and spies.

At the same time, the makeup of the agency's own workforce has changed—the CIA now selects from a wider pool than it once did when its ranks were, as I often said, "mostly white males from Yale." But the government's onerous clearance system still freezes out qualified applicants for, say, having a grandmother in Baghdad or an uncle in Tunis. Penetrating tribal and nonstate groups in the Middle East is difficult enough as it is; doing so with only a few personnel who look like the others in the targeted group, understand Arab customs, and speak a variety of Arabic dialects just adds to the danger.

While the CIA would not repeat the abuses of the post-9/11 period (described in Chapter 4), interrogations are a function better handled by the FBI, which has decades more institutional experience. We could better leverage relationships with partner intelligence services known to be highly effective at interrogations but did not use methods that violate our laws and values. Those of the United Kingdom and Israel come to mind; those of the Gulf monarchies, not so much.

Open-source intelligence, especially that gleaned from social media, will continue to gain in relevance compared to intelligence gathered by traditional methods, which tend to measure a piece of information's value by its degree of classification (and the degree of difficulty and risk involved in obtaining it). During the Cold War, nothing could match the value of a well-placed mole or a thoroughly bugged bedroom. Today, the "dip party," where spies would eavesdrop over cocktails, has gone the way of the dodo. That's in large part because much of the information policymakers seek is no longer secret. Traditional intelligence tradecraft is still applicable in the digital age—advanced cyberattacks, for example, rely on intimate knowledge of human beings, their habits, and their software use. But the CIA doesn't need an agent in the Russian Ministry of Agriculture in order to follow developments in Ukraine. Social media, in fact, has provided some of the best reports from the ground, allowing bystanders to upload photographs and videos as events unfold in real time. Now that every smartphone user is a potential collector of intelligence, the key is to skillfully sort the data. Although no structural obstacle prevents the U.S. intelligence community from doing this work well, there remains a strong bias, bordering on elitism, against using freely available information. Too often the preference is to tap terrorists' phones and send spy satellites in search of hidden training camps, not to read the tweets of a nineteen-year-old jihadist. Online radicalization often happens in plain sight, and the effects were seen on January 6 at the U.S. Capitol.

As the intelligence community moves away from traditional espionage and toward open-source analysis, one of the most important, enduring questions in the spy business will take center stage: how to protect analysis from being biased by policy preferences. The reforms that Congress enacted at the end of 2004 were the right ones for their moment. But now the terrain has shifted. Including vast reams of raw information from open sources in briefings could risk swaying policymakers with individual bits of data before analysts can present the bigger picture. There have always been ways for bias to creep into the briefing process. Analysis can be crafted with an eye toward specific policy prescriptions (e.g., regime change in Iraq). Or an agency may advance a particular policy agenda by repeatedly providing insistent briefings on a single topic that the president hasn't solicited. Ultimately, no reorganization or policy change will make bias go away, because people bring prejudices to everything they do. In the end, intelligence is only as good as the people who analyze it. That goes double for leadership.

That basic fact won't change anytime soon, but much else will. To borrow from William Gibson, the novelist who gave cyberspace its name: "The future is already here—it's just not very evenly distributed." The trends shaping the intelligence community are detectable: in budgets, in organizational charts, and in war zones. Policymakers have been slow to notice, as their attention jumps from one crisis to the next. But if Washington wants to get ahead of the curve and anticipate future flare-ups, that needs to change.

There are additional improvements that could be made to the ODNI structure and the underlying law. For example, 80 percent of intelligence spending—much of which goes to satellites—is still buried in the defense budget and thus under the control of the armed services committee. I received substantive briefings on satellite programs—but mostly as the representative of the district in which they were located, not in my HPSCI capacity. A major improvement in IRTPA is that the ODNI has authority over the "joint tasking" of satellites. This reform ensured that these expensive and individually crafted systems are focused on the highest national security priorities. Before the reform, the military services and other IC elements competed for satellite time and focus in ways that were counterproductive.

The most pressing challenge is not organizational but involves leadership and politics. HPSCI has become a partisan battleground through the Russia investigation and the first Trump impeachment. Its Senate counterpart has been more functional, and is now led by Democrats. Congress will have to step up its oversight to ensure that the IC is as proficient and adaptable as the new enemies it confronts.

FOUR

Stumbling Through the Fog of Law on Captured Terrorists

On March 7, 2002, I was part of a congressional delegation that flew to the U.S. naval base at Guantanamo Bay, Cuba (GTMO), for a tour of the new detention facility there. After landing at the airstrip, we boarded a small boat for transport across the bay to the detainee facility. A three-star army general was our guide. As we sped over the tropical water, I asked him, "How come the prison was set up here?" Without flinching, he replied, "To be beyond the reach of U.S. law." I was stunned. But I didn't speak up then, nor did I do anything about it after returning to D.C. The wire-service headline from our trip: "Detainees' Care Gets Approval; Lawmakers Give Site Thumbs Up."

Looking back, it's clear that we—and I include myself—failed to recognize the unique legal and political challenges posed by international terror suspects. After 9/11, the White House declared a law-free zone in Guantanamo and around the treatment of "high-value" detainees across the globe. Some of the worst abuses were curbed by legislation and executive order more than a decade ago. But in the absence of a comprehensive legal framework, we're

at risk of reviving some of the discredited detainee practices. A saner approach: a comprehensive legal framework
for detaining, interrogating, and trying terrorists that is
consistent with the Geneva Conventions, effective, and
politically sustainable.

Are terrorists criminals or combatants? Twenty years after
9/11 the answer is still "It depends." Today, some individuals
suspected of plotting terror attacks are arrested, informed of
their *Miranda* rights, and tried in federal courts. Others may
be detained in military facilities and tried by a military commission. Still others may be evaporated by a Hellfire missile
launched from a drone. Then, in 2016, a candidate ran for
president—and won—pledging to send more prisoners to
GTMO and promising interrogations even "tougher" than
waterboarding.

In the wake of 9/11, Bush's popularity and public fear of
another attack were at their respective peaks. Under those circumstances the administration, with bipartisan congressional
support, could have received ample authority and flexibility
under a new legal framework that allowed for vigorous but
humane interrogations, protection of classified information,
prolonged detention if needed, and swift but fair trials of
those who committed serious offenses. All of this could have
been authorized and overseen by the Congress and, likely,
upheld by the courts. White House hard-liners such as Dick
Cheney would not have liked it much—nor, frankly, would
the arch-libertarians. Such a framework would have to be

revised over time in response to legitimate legal challenges or changed security circumstances. With both political parties so invested, America could have presented a united and principled front to friends and enemies alike.

To be sure, the capture of dozens of suspected Al Qaeda militants and hundreds of Taliban fighters would have created a legal conundrum for any administration. These detainees did not fit the traditional legal categories of "criminal defendant" and "prisoner of war." The former gets a lawyer and Fifth Amendment protections against self-incrimination; the latter gets the protections of the Geneva Conventions designed for this purpose.

The Bush team correctly recognized that neither framework precisely fit the problem. But then they took the extreme position that the president's authority under Article II of the Constitution, combined with the broadly worded 2001 AUMF, gave him the power to do whatever he considered necessary to stop another terrorist attack. And because this new "war" transcended borders and spanned the divide between what were traditionally considered military and civilian domains, that power's scope was limitless.

Consequently, lawyers at the Justice Department's Office of Legal Counsel, under direction from the vice president's office, drafted top-secret memos limiting the definition of "torture" to measures causing "extensive organ failure" or "imminent death." Humane treatment and adherence to the Geneva Conventions were required only as long as they were consistent with "military necessity," which served as a giant loophole.

The legitimacy of this entire approach depended on the ability of the U.S. government to know for sure that a particular captive really was a killer or mastermind, as opposed to a lower-level foot soldier, hanger-on, or—as would sometimes turn out to be the case—a person in the wrong place at the wrong time. The absence of habeas corpus protections (the right to challenge one's detention in court) meant that detainees had no way to protest their confinement to an independent entity that, unlike the government, did not have a vested interest in presuming their guilt. Even a U.S. citizen could be plucked off the streets of an American city and designated an "unlawful combatant"—the legal definition adopted by the administration; that is exactly what happened to alleged "dirty bomber" Jose Padilla a few months later.

Administration officials would later argue that prisoners captured in previous wars—like the hundreds of thousands of German soldiers captured overseas and detained in the United States for the duration of World War II—had never been supplied with lawyers or provided with access to courts. But those conflicts had a limited duration and there was no doubt that those prisoners, captured armed and in uniform, were in fact enemy combatants. The Bush administration's legal formulation was totally one-sided: all the advantages offered by the criminal justice and prisoner-of-war systems went to the government, with none of their protections provided to those detained. Any check on interrogation methods or detention terms depended on the grace of the government, which in this instance was a handful of senior political appointees in the White House, Justice Department, and the

Pentagon. (In anticipation of their objections, secretary of state Colin Powell, State Department attorneys, and even the National Security Council were excluded from the process.)

The first sign of trouble, at least publicly, was President Bush's order on November 13, 2001, establishing military tribunals solely under his executive authority as commander in chief. For decades terrorists had been sentenced to long terms in maximum-security prisons through federal courts. Additionally, although the Geneva Convention may not have envisioned precisely the challenges the government faced with detainees after 9/11, it provided at least a starting point consistent with America's treaty obligations. And the Convention's Article III applies broadly to any conflict, including irregular wars with insurgents out of uniform. Section (1)(d), which relates to tribunals, prohibits punishment "without previous judgement by a regularly constituted court, affording all the judicial guarantees which are recognized as indispensable by civilized peoples."

The U.S. Constitution also provides significant powers with respect to detainees. The Constitution's Article I, Section 8 gives the Congress the power to make "rules concerning captures on land and water." This logically includes detention, interrogation, and trial. When I raised this issue with David Addington, Vice President Cheney's chief legal counsel, he told me dismissively this provision referred only to piracy. But the Barbary pirates were, in most respects, the equivalent of terrorists at the turn of the nineteenth century—"unlawful combatants," in the parlance of Bush's White House—and a major national security threat to the fledgling republic. "Absent authorization from Congress, the president's order is at best hollow and at worse could be misapplied," I told *Congressional Quarterly*. When challenged on the tribunals and other measures, the administration deployed what soon became the familiar tactic of asserting that such criticisms, in the words of attorney general John Ashcroft, "only aid terrorists."

Undeterred, in December 2001 my California House colleague Zoe Lofgren and I sponsored legislation requiring that military tribunals include habeas corpus rights and oversight by federal courts. I envisioned trials taking place either on American military bases overseas or on American aircraft carriers in open waters. We intended this legislation to apply only to those captured abroad for violations of the law of war in a war zone—not to people like Jose Padilla, arrested on the streets of an American city. As in the USA PATRIOT Act, which was signed into law on October 26, 2001, we proposed a sunset clause after four years. We also tied the use of tribunals more closely to the AUMF passed by the Congress three days after the 9/11 attacks. This would exclude any prisoners not associated with Al Qaeda, even if they were terrorists (e.g., the Tamil Tigers in Sri Lanka or Basque separatists in Spain).

Our bill went nowhere. But it was a statement early on that Congress would not be an idle bystander as a new wartime regime took root. According to a contemporaneous *New York Times* poll, the public at that time favored traditional criminal trials for captured terrorists over military tribunals by 50 percent to 40 percent. It turned out the American people had a more balanced perspective than we in Washington gave them credit for.

Looking back on the excesses and abuses committed in the aftermath of 9/11, it is all too convenient to say that no one could have foreseen what would happen. As with later claims about Iraqi WMD, there were warnings sounded by voices in the political and bureaucratic wilderness. The first major legal challenge to the administration's detention policies came in February 2002. A coalition of pacifist clergy in California led by former attorney general Ramsey Clark challenged the administration's assertion that detainees at GTMO had no constitutional rights because they were "unlawful combatants." The suit was thrown out quickly for lack of standing; the plaintiffs needed to produce an actual person who had been wronged by the government. The judge wrote: "That question is NOT before this Court and nothing in this ruling suggests that the captives are entitled to no legal protection whatsoever."

The case was a blip in the headlines at the time, but we should have paid closer attention to the administration's response. Prior Supreme Court decisions had permitted the use of military tribunals during armed conflict. But instead of arguing the merits, the administration claimed that detainees had no legal rights because GTMO—under lease from Cuba—was not sovereign U.S. territory. As a matter of law and common sense this reasoning was strained at best. Early on I recognized that it would be near impossible to persuade the administration to change its position. So I focused on the legislative route.

Successful legal challenges to the detention policies came later. The names Rasul, Hamdi, Hamdan, Boumediene, and others are now inscribed in the history of U.S. jurisprudence. The administration would lose each case—albeit narrowly—before the Supreme Court. The tragic irony is that the White House ended up in a far weaker position in terms of its authority to detain such individuals than if it had worked with Congress from the start.

Captured fighters deemed to be Al Qaeda or high-ranking Taliban—too valuable and dangerous to house in Afghanistan—began arriving in GTMO in January 2002. Their first destination was the hastily erected Camp X-Ray, which had open-air holding cells with chain-link sides topped by a tin roof. The pictures released by the U.S. military—and published worldwide—made the facility look like cages at a zoo. My subcommittee's visit in March was part of the administration's outreach to reassure Congress not only that conditions were much improved but also to convince us that a more permanent facility was necessary to protect the American people and collect vital intelligence. The delegation consisted of seven members of the House Intelligence Subcommittee on Terrorism and Homeland Security, led by Saxby Chambliss as chair and me as ranking member. Saxby spoke for most of us when he said: "These 300 detainees are the worst of the bad guys. . . . They are mean, mean people, and we need to get every bit of information that we can from them." Later that summer I told CNN, "I think we need to be doing more to question those prisoners down there and get information about the next wave of attacks." I was a strong proponent of interrogation to gain intelligence— about enemy intentions, organizations, practices, and, above all, the possible attacks. But I never imagined the United States would engage in so-called enhanced interrogation methods amounting to torture. In retrospect, it was the logical, if grotesque, consequence of a White House operating without congressional and judicial boundaries.

In February 2003 I was briefed on the interrogations of senior Al Qaeda militants who had been captured to date (Khalid Sheikh Mohammed [KSM], the 9/11 mastermind, was captured the following month in Pakistan). The CIA described using "enhanced" methods to generate more intelligence from Abu Zubaydah, then believed to be a high-ranking Al Qaeda leader (the CIA did not mention it had withheld treatment for Zubaydah's wounds in order to ratchet up the pressure on him to talk). The descriptions were purposely vague, referring to "applications"—as if the prisoner were putting on lipstick. But it was clear these techniques were pushing well beyond what the United States had permitted before as a matter of official policy. The CIA general counsel said that Zubaydah's interrogation had been videotaped but that the tape would be destroyed after the CIA inspector general completed his inquiry.

The interrogations being described by the CIA general counsel and the stated intent to destroy the video were both

1977: Walking with President Jimmy Carter and Jack Watson between the White House and the Executive Office Building. I was Jack's deputy.

1984: With then-Congresswoman Geraldine Ferraro, who was the first female vice presidential candidate on a major party ticket. I served as outside counsel to the Democratic Platform Committee, which she chaired, and we became fast friends.

1993: Surrounded by my family as Speaker Tom Foley administers the Oath of Office as I enter Congress.

1993: Meeting Israeli Prime Minister Yitzhak Rabin during one of my many visits to the region.

1994: Visiting the aerospace firm TRW with then–Vice President Al Gore. My congressional district was central to the production of America's intelligence satellites.

1994: Demonstrating bipartisan support in my first reelection to Congress.

1995: On a visit to Bosnia as a second-term member of Congress.

1998: Standing with then-President Bill Clinton, whose first term focused more on domestic issues and less on a post–Cold War national security strategy.

2001: Breakfast with the Dalai Lama and Senators Dianne Feinstein and Hillary Clinton and Rep. Ellen Tauscher.

2004: President Bush signs into law the Intelligence Reform and Terrorism Prevention Act. In addition to me, he is surrounded (front row) by Pete Hoekstra, Susan Collins, Tom Kean, Joe Lieberman, and Bill Frist.

2005: Secretary of Homeland Security Michael Chertoff and I forged a friendship that lasts to this day. Here we are running along Venice Beach on one of his visits to key security sites in my congressional district.

2005: On a CODEL to the tribal areas of Pakistan, dressed in local garb.

2008: George Bush invited me to travel on Air Force One to visit Robinson Helicopter factory in my congressional district. We are chatting in his private office on board the plane.

To Jane Harman
With best wishes,
G. Bush

2008: Standing next to my friend Congresswoman Heather Wilson at the signing ceremony for the FISA Amendments Act at the White House.

2009: Visiting with CENTCOM Commander General David Petraeus in Tampa as part of a Homeland Security Committee CODEL to Guantanamo Bay, Cuba, that I led.

2010: President Obama signs into law the Reducing Overclassification Act that I authored.

2011: Mexican President Enrique Pena Nieto speaks at the Wilson Center during my first week there. Here he is meeting Sidney Harman, on what would be his first and last visit to the Center before his death a month later.

2011: CIA Director Dave Petraeus surprised and honored me with his personal Director's Award.

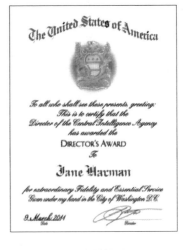

The United States of America

To all who shall see these presents, greeting:
This is to certify that the
Director of the Central Intelligence Agency
has awarded the
DIRECTOR'S AWARD
To
Jane Harman

for extraordinary Fidelity and Essential Service
Given under my hand in the City of Washington D.C.

9 March 2011

2011: Speaker John Boehner and I forged a cordial relationship. He spoke at my farewell party in the Capitol.

2015: Madeleine Albright and I were staffers on Capitol Hill and in the Carter White House and remained friends during her illustrious career as UN Ambassador and as Secretary of State. A regular visitor at the Wilson Center, she credits Wilson with securing the independence of her native Czechoslovakia.

2018: At a meeting of the Munich Security Conference Advisory Council. The other woman in the photo is German Defense Minister Ursula von der Leyen who is now President of the European Commission.

2018: On the 50th anniversary of the Wilson Center, Dr. Henry Kissinger received the Woodrow Wilson Award for Public Service. He often spoke at the Center, where the China program is named the Kissinger Institute on China and the United States.

2018: At the same awards gala, the Wilson Center honored House Majority Leader Steny Hoyer and Republican Senate Majority Whip Roy Blunt for bipartisanship.

2018: Arguing the proposition "The House Believes the War on Terror Has Been Its Own Worst Enemy" at the Oxford Union.

2019: Christine Lagarde came to Washington as IMF Managing Director just as I became President of the Wilson Center. She and I became close friends. Here we are at the Milken Institute Global Conference.

strongly disturbing to me. Because this information was highly classified, I could not talk to anyone about it except for the one HPSCI staffer who was present at the briefing. She helped me draft a top-secret letter, since declassified, to the CIA general counsel, urging him not to destroy the Zubaydah videotape. The letter said the preserved video "would be the best proof that the written record is accurate, if such record is called into question in the future. The fact of destruction would reflect badly on the Agency." With respect to the interrogation techniques, I wrote:

> I would like to know what kind of policy review took place and what questions were examined. In particular, I would like to know whether the most senior levels of the White House have determined that these practices are consistent with the principles and policies of the United States. Have enhanced techniques been authorized and approved by the President?

The response drafted by the CIA general counsel, Scott Muller—which was never sent to me but I saw years later—was the bureaucratic equivalent of a brush-off: "While I do not think it appropriate for me to comment on issues that are a matter of policy, much less the nature and extent of Executive Branch policy deliberations, I think it would be fair to assume that policy as well as legal matters have been addressed within the Executive Branch."

I would later become the subject of both praise and criticism for this exchange. Praise, because I was the only member of the Congress to raise any kind of formal written objection at the time. Criticism, because I had not condemned the interrogation techniques themselves, only raised the issue of whether there was policy guidance from the White House. I had hoped—unrealistically, in retrospect—for a constructive dialogue with the administration on the topic. I would learn later that the CIA destroyed the Zubaydah tapes in 2005, following media exposure of other detainee abuses. The order was given by Jose Rodriguez, the head of the Agency's clandestine division. The order was carried out by Gina Haspel, then a senior CIA official overseeing the "black sites" and later director of the CIA in the Trump administration.

Like most Americans, the first time I saw the Abu Ghraib photographs was in the news media. The same was true for the chairs and ranking members of the House and Senate Armed Services Committees. And, it turns out, for the president of the United States. Apart from the moral outrage caused by the images—which included naked Iraqi prisoners being taunted by grinning soldiers and terrorized by dogs—this scandal showcased just how poorly the Iraq War was being managed. Members of Congress were later shown the full set of photos—more than 1,800 over three hours—most of which were never seen by the public. The usually garrulous members came out of the briefing room silent and ashen-faced. I told the press, "The world is tuned in and America is on trial. Congress will be on trial too if it doesn't act."

The armed services committees had principal responsibility for Congress's response. With Duncan Hunter, a strong White House ally, in charge, it was unlikely any real accountability would come from the House. In contrast, Senator John Warner of Virginia, who chaired the Senate Armed Services Committee, had served in the navy and marines during World War II and Korea, later becoming secretary of the navy under President Nixon. Next in seniority to Warner was John McCain, whose suffering as a prisoner of war in Vietnam had long been part of American military lore. More junior, but never shy, was Lindsey Graham. Graham was also an Air Force Reserve JAG officer with close ties to the military legal community, most of whom opposed what their civilian Pentagon bosses were doing to detainees. Principled bipartisan oversight would come from this important Senate committee.

The intelligence committees had a secondary oversight role, but an important one. We would learn soon that the undersecretary of defense for intelligence, Steve Cambone—DoD's senior representative to the intelligence community—had ordered the commander of GTMO, Major General Geoffrey Miller, to inspect detainee operations in Iraq; some feared he would "Gitmoize" them. House Intelligence Committee chair Porter Goss seemed in no hurry to embarrass or antagonize the administration. On May 20, more than two weeks after the scandal broke, we received a classified briefing by General Miller on detainee practices in Abu Ghraib. The briefing was inadequate—we were learning more from the news media at that point—and I admonished Miller for the "gaps and discrepancies" in his presentation and for selectively withholding information. He would draft a follow-up response with additional information, but the administration's credibility—including, sadly, much of the senior military leadership's—was pretty much shot. I told *USA Today* in June 2004 that "oversight is on life support over here" (in the House). Our committee and armed services had by then seen several classified briefings, "but the story has to be told to the public." Duncan Hunter stated that he was "outraged by the outrage" caused by what took place at Abu Ghraib. As far as Hunter was concerned, it was up to the military to deal with the few "bad apples."

The White House claimed Abu Ghraib was a Pentagon problem. Rumsfeld by then was a convenient lightning rod for Iraq criticism. The Pentagon political leadership would, in turn, try to blame the army. The only outside investigation—led by former defense secretaries James Schlesinger and Harold Brown—concluded it was "Animal House on the night shift." The rationale was that the Abu Ghraib behavior was so outrageous—sophomoric as well as cruel—that it couldn't possibly have been officially sanctioned. With respect to the specific acts depicted in the photos, that was largely true. But there was still plenty for the Pentagon leadership to answer for.

The irony was clear. On the one hand, U.S. troops were instructed officially that the Geneva Conventions applied to Iraq. On the other hand, the White House and Pentagon leaders declared those fighting the United States in Iraq to be terrorists like those who attacked us on 9/11. U.S. soldiers handling Iraqi detainees—most of them National Guard members who had never expected to be on long deployments—were soon overwhelmed. It was known in the U.S. military and IC that special operators and the CIA were using harsher techniques when it came to "high-value" Al Qaeda suspects. In October 2003 the commander in Baghdad signed off on a new "interrogation and counter-resistance" policy for all of Iraq that transgressed traditional U.S. military practices. Given the rhetoric and changing guidance, abuse was not only possible but inevitable.

What followed was a raft of internal Pentagon investigations led by general officers up to three stars who examined certain aspects of detainee operations but never strayed outside their lanes—or above their rank. In response to public outrage, the administration would release (or leak) a series of documents that summer showing the evolution of interrogations since 9/11. In a process akin to peeling back an onion, we would learn how policies and practices migrated—sometimes by word of mouth—from CIA black sites to GTMO and eventually to Iraq. In one of the memos that were released, Rumsfeld complained that too many low-level Taliban were being sent to GTMO, undermining the administration's earlier assertions—and, frankly, my own—that it housed only the "worst of the worst" and those possessing valuable intelligence. As it turns out, during my first GTMO visit in 2002 defense officials were already frustrated that so little good information was coming out of the detainees. A top-secret CIA analysis that summer concluded that few of the GTMO prisoners had real intelligence value. The top Al Qaeda guys—the real "worst of the worst"—were being held by the CIA at black sites. But instead of adjusting to reality, the administration doubled down. Interrogations became more intense and aggressive. When they didn't produce the wanted results, requests went up the chain for even harsher methods.

Rumsfeld signed memoranda first approving, then rescinding after internal protests, then approving again, harsher interrogations for recalcitrant GTMO detainees. The list of techniques, arrayed in neat bullet points, referred to removing clothing, prolonged standing, stress positions, sleep deprivation, and "fear up" involving dogs. It was presented to sound reasonable, including requirements for a full "interrogation plan" and constant medical supervision. Rumsfeld even complained they seemed too soft; he scribbled on one of the memos that he typically was on his feet eight to twelve hours per day, so why should a detainee only be forced to stand for four?

The main subject of the new DoD interrogation "stress matrix" was in fact a serious Al Qaeda bad guy. Mohammed Al-Qahtani, a would-be "twentieth hijacker" prevented from entering the United States, was picked up in the fall of 2001 by Pakistani intelligence, turned over to the U.S. military, and brought to GTMO. We would learn later that Qahtani was stripped naked, blasted with loud music, and forbidden to sleep for days at a time. Female military personnel were used to upset the religious sensibilities of this devout Muslim, and women's lingerie was draped on his head. The sophomoric aspect of this treatment was highlighted by the Pentagon later to divert attention from the real abuse tak-

ing place. In what was a familiar scenario, the tactics strayed
quickly from the approved list—in terms of method, duration, and intensity—as zealous and frustrated interrogators
pressed for more.

Ultimately, waterboarding and the worst CIA practices
were never approved for GTMO. Nonetheless, the Pentagon-
approved techniques used on Qahtani caused his heart rate
to drop to dangerously low levels, requiring that he be hos-
pitalized. Already mentally ill, he was found curled in a ball
having pulled out much of his hair. He would later attempt
suicide multiple times. Not only was Qahtani useless for intelligence purposes, but his brutal treatment made it impossible to try him in federal court. Qahtani would join a handful
of detainees with the dubious distinction of being too dangerous to release but too abused to prosecute.

In his second inaugural address President Bush said: "America's vital interests and our deepest beliefs are now one. . . . It is
the policy of the United States to seek and support the growth
of democratic movements and institutions in every nation
and culture, with the ultimate goal of ending tyranny in our
world." The speech was beautifully written—but conveyed a
startling level of hubris about America's power to shape events
around the globe. And in one respect it rang hollow, considering the administration's unwillingness to consider any systematic change to its detainee policies. By that point Bush's
attorney general nominee, Alberto Gonzales, had provided
written answers to the Senate Judiciary Committee stating
that intelligence officials acting abroad were not required to
abide by constitutional provisions banning "cruel, unusual,

and inhumane treatment." He then softened that position in testimony. In response, I said: "President Bush's inaugural address rightly focused on the importance of promoting liberty and respect for human dignity. Yet those principles will be undermined unless the United States addresses the serious matter of how we detain and interrogate individuals in our custody." With respect to Gonzales's statements, I added, "If his interpretation is correct, it is evidence of a major gap in U.S. law."

It was a gap I was determined to close with H.R. 3985, the Interrogation Procedures Act. I previewed it in a speech at Georgetown University Law School in February 2005. To avoid sanctimony and hectoring, I positioned the detainee issue as a complex problem—the "fog of law"—for the executive and legislative branches to solve working together. My proposed bill defined torture according to the accepted international definition in the Geneva Conventions of "severe pain or suffering"—not the exquisitely narrow definitions in the opinions from the Department of Justice's Office of Legal Counsel (OLC). The Abu Ghraib and GTMO revelations had revived what were thought to be previously settled debates over the morality and efficacy of torture—with some people, such as political commentator Charles Krauthammer, arguing it was effective and in some cases absolutely necessary. Notorious agencies such as the Nazi Gestapo and Soviet KGB probably gained usable information from their most sadistic practices. But nothing in recent history showed that the results came anywhere close to justifying the moral and strategic costs for Western democracies, whether one considers the British in Northern Ireland, the French in Algeria, the Israelis with Palestinian terrorists, or, as we would learn the hard way, the United States after 9/11. "The weight of academic and field research indicates that torturing a prisoner does not often elicit useful intelligence." The U.S. military, to its credit, scrambled to reestablish lawful detainee practices. Yet, as I noted, the administration still maintained that the president could authorize "cruel techniques against foreigners abroad with few restrictions and virtually no oversight."

At the time of the Georgetown speech I continued to believe that some of the coercive CIA interrogations had in fact "yielded vital information." We knew that the CIA had been employing waterboarding and other brutal methods since 2002. The twisted and amateurish origins of these techniques were only divulged years later: retired air force psychologists had been paid tens of millions of dollars to reverse-engineer North Korean and other Soviet-bloc methods. These techniques had been used by the U.S. military in training to prepare pilots for harsh treatment if captured. The frequency and intensity of the use of the harshest methods—more than 180 waterboarding "applications" for KSM—were far greater than we were led to believe. We would also learn about "walling," "use of insects," "mock burial," and more. The justifications provided by the White House and CIA when the gruesome details came out turned out to be pretty thin. In almost every case the information obtained was no longer useful or could have been obtained by other means.

_____

Later that summer the Pentagon launched a public relations offensive showcasing the "kinder and gentler" GTMO. The DoD public affairs shop produced a handout describing in detail the quality of meals being served. Administration surrogates would answer nearly every question about detainees with a reference to "honey-glazed chicken" or "lemon-baked fish." While this is easy to mock today, they had a point: conditions had greatly improved. The detainees were apparently gaining weight, and they had access to libraries and extensive religious accommodations. No one was being harmed absent a deliberate provocation to the guards, and serious interrogations were pretty much over. What little information the detainees might have known had long ceased to be useful, though the White House and Pentagon continued to claim otherwise.

Irrespective of how well the prisoners were eating, I still saw a major gap in the law and oversight. Discussing GTMO at a session of the 9/11 Public Discourse Project in June 2005, I said, "Congressional oversight did not work. We asked all the right questions; we did not get the right answers." In part that was what the bill I described in the Georgetown speech was trying to fix. It helped lay the groundwork for the Detainee Treatment Act, introduced by Senator John McCain. McCain's bill was far from ideal, from my perspective; for one thing, it limited the ability of detainees to appeal their status beyond review panels controlled by the U.S military. Nonetheless, it was a strong statement by America's legislative branch against torture, prohibiting "cruel, inhuman, or degrading treatment or punishment" of *any* U.S. government prisoner. It also showed that Congress had a pulse regarding its constitutional responsibilities, at least in this one area of national security. The challenge the Detainee Treatment Act faced was not from Democrats—despite some reservations, we were nearly unanimous in support—but from the White House, in particular the Office of the Vice President, and its most stalwart supporters in the House. The president initially pushed for more carve-outs exempting the CIA from restrictions, but eventually he bowed to reality. Plus the Senate vote was 90 to 9, which was well beyond the numbers needed for a veto override. Bush included a signing statement—almost certainly drafted by Addington—saying:

> The executive branch shall construe . . . in a manner consistent with the constitutional authority of the President to supervise the unitary executive branch and as Commander in Chief and consistent with the constitutional limitations on the judicial power, which will assist in achieving the shared objective of the Congress and the President . . . of protecting the American people from further terrorist attacks.

Translation: The White House would interpret and execute the law as it saw fit, to include extrajudicial mistreatment of detainees. It was the "military necessity" loophole all over again.

The Detainee Treatment Act was a step in the right direction. It still left in place much of the White House's post-9/11
extrajudicial apparatus for handling detainees. The Supreme
Court struck down much of that apparatus in June 2006 with
the *Hamdan* decision, ruling the military commissions set up
by the administration to be unconstitutional. In her opinion
for the Court, Justice Sandra Day O'Connor famously wrote,
"A state of war is not a blank check for the President." That
fall the Republican congressional leadership—this time with
White House support—began drafting legislation to provide
a legal framework for the administration's detainee policies,
in response to *Hamdan*. Up to that point my main concern
had been the complete absence of congressional involvement.
Now we were faced with a situation in which the Republican majority was trying to codify egregious practices. My
views began to diverge from those of many of my GOP
colleagues—including Senator McCain, John Warner, and
Lindsey Graham—with whom I'd shared common cause on
Abu Ghraib and GTMO. Their primary concern, as veterans
on the armed services committee, was the impact of abusive
practices on the reputation and character of the U.S. military.
The process for determining detention status and trying war
crimes was less of a priority. The White House decided to
ignore HPSCI and rushed through a "take it or leave it" bill
that would grant the CIA exceptions from the requirement
to comply with the Army Field Manual. In a September
2006 statement opposing the latest iteration of the Military
Commissions Act, I said the president was "rolling out a program designed to force members of Congress in a box, either

you support an 85-page bill that expands executive power or you're coddling terrorists. I resent that."

In the next Congress, I would continue to work on these issues as chair of the Homeland Security Subcommittee on Intelligence. Wasting little time in this new role, in March I joined Jerry Nadler, the new Democratic chair of the House Judiciary Committee, and eighty-six co-sponsors on bills that would fix some of the serious flaws of the Military Commissions Act, enacted six months earlier. Along with companion legislation in the Senate, the bills narrowed the definition of "unlawful enemy combatant" to those individuals who directly participated in hostilities against the United States or who had aided in the 9/11 attacks. Evidence obtained through coercion or hearsay was banned. The jurisdiction of the federal courts—removed by the Military Commission Act for detainees' habeas petitions—was reinstated. Inhumane treatment and the denial of the right to trial were punishable under the U.S. War Crimes Act.

The last two years of the Bush administration—dominated by the Iraq surge and economic crises—were mostly a period of stasis on detainees, with spots of progress. The Supreme Court's *Boumediene* decision in 2008 would overturn much of the Military Commissions Act as unconstitutional (as many of us had predicted). The adjudication of GTMO detainees was thrown back into limbo, where it has pretty much stayed. As a practical matter, the Bush administration made GTMO a less visible problem by drawing down the population—from more than 700 at its peak, it had been reduced to less than 250 by the end of 2008.

Barack Obama campaigned on a pledge to turn the page on the
Bush-era war on terror: getting out of Iraq, fixing Afghanistan, and restoring the country's moral leadership by banning
torture and closing GTMO. His rhetoric was welcome, but
deciding how to handle detainees going forward would prove
vexing for Congress and the new administration. On January
9, 2009—days before Obama's inauguration—I joined senior
Democratic leaders of the House Judiciary Committee to introduce a bill establishing strict guidelines for interrogations
by all government agencies. It was designed to eliminate any
possible opening for torture provided by prior legislation or
Bush's signing statements. Most significantly, our bill also required the closure of GTMO within one year and authorized
options to try or transfer the remaining detainees.

On Obama's second day in office, he signed an executive
order reflecting much of what was in the House legislation:
banning torture or cruel and inhumane treatment by any
part of the U.S. government, including intelligence agencies. To deal with senior terrorists captured overseas who
genuinely had intelligence value, the administration set
up the High-Value Detainee Interrogation Group (HIG),
a three-agency entity—FBI, CIA, and DoD—bringing
together the nation's top professionals in intelligence and
interrogation. In an important shift, the HIG was led by
the FBI, reinforcing the primacy of U.S. law in guiding
interrogations.

I supported the HIGs and the substance of what the
Obama administration was pursuing. Despite the important

change in tone, Obama's approach to interrogations recommended reforms that were already in place. CIA interrogations using the most egregious techniques had been halted in 2004. Black sites had been closed in 2006. However, there was nothing preventing a future president, under dire circumstances, from reverting to abusive treatment by the CIA (or another element of government) in the name of "military necessity." That is why Congress was so important.

On his second day in office Obama also signed an executive order closing GTMO. The famously deliberative Obama made the decision first and counted on his team to figure out the implementation later. I was optimistic at the beginning: "Yes, closing Guantanamo is going to be hard, but I think the year framework is realistic." It appeared that most of the GTMO detainee cases could be resolved in U.S. courts, either civilian or military. The remaining cases might require legislation establishing special procedures for trying and holding the prisoners. There was enormous goodwill for this new president, and Democrats had a strong majority in the House and a nearly veto-proof majority in the Senate.

The Obama administration established the Guantanamo Review Task Force, which stalled quickly. For one thing, GTMO had been set up primarily for interrogations outside the reach of law, not to prepare suspects for trial—criminal, tribunal, or otherwise. With 500 detainees already released by the Bush administration, those left at GTMO were the toughest cases. There still had not been a real effort to come to terms with the way we gathered intelligence after 9/11. Reflecting later on detainee policies across the Bush and

Obama administrations, I wrote in *Foreign Policy* in March 2012 that "the result is a hodgepodge of internally inconsistent policies, an outsized role for the courts . . . and huge gaps in what the public knows and has been told."

What had been a consensus view that GTMO was a black eye for the United States and should close quickly became a PR disaster. Both 2008 Republican nominee McCain and Bush 43 (at the end of his second term) favored closure. But trying to close GTMO would prove difficult. The attorney general's announcement—not vetted fully beforehand with either the White House or Congress— that the 9/11 culprits would be tried in downtown Manhattan created a predictable firestorm of opposition, led by Mayor Michael Bloomberg. On the substance, the White House was right: the worst GTMO prisoners, the 9/11 plotters especially, should be brought to justice in an American courtroom, for the world to see. But the politics and rollout were a mess. The Obama White House discovered that most Americans, even if appalled by the torture scandals and fed up with the Iraq War, were far more willing to accept GTMO's continued operation if the alternative was bringing the accused terrorists to a location nearby.

In October 2010, the flailing effort to try KSM in New York suffered another political setback. A Tanzanian named Ahmed Ghailani, involved in the 1998 embassy bombings, received a not-guilty verdict in more than 220 counts in federal court, while being convicted of just one. Critics of the administration pointed to this as an example of why trying

Al Qaeda leaders in U.S. courts was too risky. What if, after all, they were acquitted? In a statement I pointed out that Ghailani would likely face between twenty years and life in a secure supermax federal prison for that one count alone. Indeed, it was a stiffer sentence than all but one of the sentences meted out by the GTMO military tribunals. Between 2001 and 2010 there had been nearly 1,000 indictments on terrorism charges, 90 percent of which led to convictions. Only five detainees had been convicted in military tribunals, and two of those convicted by a tribunal had already been set free. Ghailani would have been convicted on more counts were it not for some evidence being ruled inadmissible because of his prior interrogation and treatment. In a November 2010 statement I said, "More than 200 years of American jurisprudence and a clear track record of success should not be thrown out the window or falsely characterized for political advantage." Nonetheless, strong bipartisan majorities in the Congress would repeatedly vote for language in defense authorization bills preventing the closure of GTMO, moving any of the prisoners to the United States for trial or confinement, or transferring them to third countries. "Congress first spooked itself and then launched a politically expedient campaign to scare the American people by invoking visions of grisly terrorist killers wandering around their neighborhoods. It's the Willie Horton ad campaign all over again," I commented.

Regardless of where the detainees would be held, more fundamental questions persisted through the Obama presidency, extending beyond my tenure in the Congress. Does "preventive detention" square with the Constitution and American values? Should the Geneva Conventions—which specify procedures for capture and imprisonment of enemy combatants—be updated? Four years after leaving the Congress, I tried to address some of these questions with Jack Goldsmith, a Harvard Law professor who had served as a voice of sanity in the Justice Department's Office of Legal Counsel under Bush 43. He and I wrote an opinion piece for the *Washington Post* in February 2015 acknowledging that "Guantanamo should be closed but not until the president presents a realistic plan and makes his case to Congress and the nation." With respect to the remaining "high-risk" prisoners, we said, "Transferring the detainees to the United States is an opportunity to strengthen the legal basis for their long-term detention," which was becoming increasingly fraught as the armed conflict in Afghanistan (where most of the GTMO detainees were captured) wound down. We called for legislation that could supplement the military rationale for holding non-prosecutable but very dangerous terrorists with a form of administrative detention akin to civil commitment. Such a statute could prescribe the definition of "dangerousness" that warrants detention, the processes for determining a continued threat to public safety over time, and the standards for judicial review. We thought it was the "least bad option for dealing with detainees."

By January 2015 there were some fifty GTMO detainees the administration had determined were no longer dangerous, but relocating them to their home or third countries was complicated. The bulk releases of detainees near the end of the Bush years had produced cases of former prisoners taking up arms against the United States. As we would learn later, several of those released rejoined the Taliban, providing fodder for advocates of the Cheney-Addington approach. Five of the most senior Taliban still being held were freed in May 2014 by the Obama administration in exchange for the captured U.S. Army soldier Bo Bergdahl. They would become, ironically or fortuitously, part of the Taliban team negotiating with the United States in Qatar to end our military presence in Afghanistan.

Today, we still have not solved the problem of how to handle detainees in the post-9/11 world, but the steps Congress could take to remove the fog of law are quite clear. A twenty-first-century approach to detained combatants could create a legal framework to address four issues: (1) the "ticking time bomb" scenario; (2) rules and procedures for the operation of the High-Value Detainee Interrogation Group (HIG); (3) the concept of "preventive detention"; and (4) the application of Article III of the Geneva Conventions to what have been called "unlawful combatants."

The most fraught issue is the "ticking time bomb" scenario, when the the prisoner is known to have a piece of information about a grievously harmful attack. Congress has outlawed torture, and the CIA is not going to repeat the mistakes of its enhanced interrogation program. But under such dire circumstances, with many lives hanging in the balance, interrogators need very specific guidance and assurance that they are operating lawfully. More than fifteen years ago, in my Georgetown speech, I proposed legislation that, while clearly banning torture, would have permitted techniques that were coercive but did not "shock the conscience." Their use would have to be reported immediately to the attorney general and briefed to the Congress. My views have since evolved—though others argued this from the beginning—and I now believe that any legal wiggle room on harsh interrogations creates a "slippery slope" toward their inevitable use. Indeed, it is often unclear at the onset of an interrogation if in fact the situation is one of a "ticking time bomb" and whether or not the prisoner has lifesaving knowledge. Under such circumstances, the understandable instinct is to lean toward "better safe than sorry." As with any weapon of armed conflict (short of strategic nuclear weapons), having the techniques available invariably means that they will be used at some point.

The laws of any country are, at the end of the day, an expression of what is right and wrong. By allowing even a semblance of torture—even with all the caveats and safeguards described earlier—America would effectively be sanctioning it. The better option is to outlaw enhanced interrogation procedures. If, under an exceedingly rare and anguishing scenario, the interrogating professionals conclude that an abusive technique may provide lifesaving information, the president can make the call whether to break the law. He or she will then need to explain that decision to the country and take the consequences. As unsatisfying as that scenario is from a policy or legal perspective, it is better than the alternative. If it seems outlandish to think torture could make a comeback, consider that as late as 2016 a candidate won the presidency saying we must "fight fire with fire" by using waterboarding and even killing the families of terrorist suspects.

Second, a new statutory framework should include rules and procedures to govern the operation of the High-Value Detainee Interrogation Group, first established by the Obama administration as an alternative to the discredited CIA program. For noncitizens who are detained overseas and who are considered to pose a threat of attack on the United States or to have valuable knowledge of terrorist plans and operations, the law should permit a limited period of time (thirty days) to detain and question the suspects in a location outside the protection of U.S. law (likely a ship on the high seas). Once that period is up, the United States would have to make a determination whether to turn these individuals over to their own country's government. If that is not feasible—if, say, the detainee was a citizen of a failed state such as Yemen or Libya—and if still considered of high intelligence value or too dangerous to release, the detainee would be brought back to the United States for preventive detention.

Third, those individuals moved into preventive detention in the United States—people such as KSM (assuming GTMO is closed) or HIG detainees—would have their cases reviewed on a periodic basis (every year) by an independent federal court. How and where this preventive detention takes place would, obviously, be a sticking point. Parochial concerns about safety doomed an effort to transfer GTMO detainees to the United States a decade ago. A hardened military facility in a remote part of the continental United States makes the most sense. For the 9/11 plotters and the most self-evidently dangerous prisoners, a supermax prison may be required.

Fourth, there is the role of the Geneva Conventions, famously called "quaint" by Bush White House lawyers. It's noteworthy that the sticking point for the 1977 update of Geneva's Article III—according to Carter administration lawyers who worked on it—dealt with the eligibility of members of terror groups like the Palestine Liberation Organization or the Irish Republican Army for prisoner-of-war status. Bush officials would later claim that affording Geneva Conventions protections to individuals they called "unlawful combatants"—those not wearing uniforms or carrying weapons openly—would effectively reward those individuals for violating the laws of war. The Geneva Conventions are broad enough to handle this category of insurgents and even terrorists, and Congress should make clear that it applies.

Another tough issue—outside the reach of U.S. law—relates to thousands of ISIS captives from many countries who are being held in camps in northern Syria. It is not clear how they could be charged or tried criminally. Many of their home countries refuse to take them. Given the level of brutality and fanaticism associated with ISIS, these prisoners as a group could not be turned loose. It will take a coordinated international effort to deal with this problem.

During the 2000s many detainee practices were overturned by the U.S. Supreme Court, with the Court's moderates providing swing votes. Today's Court is more starkly divided and decidedly more conservative, especially on matters of the president's commander-in-chief authority. In fact, one of the new justices, Brett Kavanaugh, was White House staff secretary during controversial detainee decisions. Looking ahead, we need to show, in a way that everyone both in the United States and globally can understand, how America's values are expressed through our policies on counterterrorism interrogation, detention, and adjudication. Kicking the can further down the road means that our adversaries can frame us as hypocrites and can continue to use GTMO and Abu Ghraib—as well as the accidental killings of civilians in drone strikes—as recruiting tools for the next generation of terrorists. The way to overcome the appeal of jihadism is to provide a better alternative. The Soviet Union and global communism ultimately collapsed for a variety of reasons— above all that the Soviet system and its satellite governments were based on lies about history, economics, and human nature. So too is the jihadist extremist ideology, albeit in different ways—it is based on lies about the value of human life, the role of women, and freedom of conscience. But America can't expose these lies with a better narrative if we aren't credibly living our values. It must be demonstrated to young people in the Muslim world who may be uneducated, unemployed, and alienated that there is a better way. It's critical for the United States to lead by example.

FIVE

Pitting Liberty Against Security
(Ben Franklin Was Right)

"You was slimed," said Illinois Republican Mark Kirk to me as I walked onto the House floor. It was April 20, 2009. That day's *New York Times* front page had run a headline above the fold: "Lawmaker Is Said to Have Agreed to Aid Lobbyists." I was the lawmaker subjected to this baseless allegation. Aspects of this convoluted narrative—involving the American Israel Public Affairs Committee (AIPAC), a flailing federal prosecution, and my interest in becoming HPSCI chair—had surfaced briefly in the press years earlier. That story went nowhere once vetted by serious media outlets. But this *Times* article carried a more explosive development: that my conversations with AIPAC had been recorded by an NSA wiretap. Outraged at both the invasion of privacy and the assault on my integrity, I wrote to the attorney general, Eric Holder, and called on the Justice Department to release all the "relevant transcripts" in "non-redacted form." I had my office and home phone swept for bugs and was relieved to find none. The assistant attorney general for national security soon released a letter affirming that I had never been the target of an investigation. Ditto from the House Ethics Committee.

That a prominent defender of lawful NSA surveillance (emphasis on "lawful") would be wiretapped by the feds was a delicious irony for some people. But this episode raised questions larger than my political fortunes: How many other members of Congress were having their conversations secretly recorded by the government? And was this eavesdropping authority being misused against the American people more broadly?

Ben Franklin wrote: "He who would trade essential liberty for a little temporary safety deserves neither liberty or safety." The legal framework for the surveillance of foreigners suspected of plotting to attack the United States had become outdated in the face of evolving technology. After 9/11 the White House implemented a new secret collection program, disregarding the Foreign Intelligence Surveillance Act (FISA) and the Constitution's Fourth Amendment. After the public revelation of massive domestic metadata collection, Congress updated FISA to address new technologies and to bring the White House program into compliance with provisions that sunset every five years. The Senate in 2019 passed a well-crafted legislative compromise to reauthorize the expiring provisions, but the House failed to act. A veto threat by former President Trump caused the House to take the bill off the calendar.

———

I've said often that the United States was trying to fight a digital enemy with an analog government. In no other area of statecraft was this truer than in electronic surveillance. The existing U.S. surveillance apparatus—designed during the Cold War with other nation-states in mind—was inadequate to deal with a stateless and tech-savvy enemy. Nor did the accompanying legal framework, principally FISA, reflect the capabilities of electronic communications in the twenty-first century.

I was on President Jimmy Carter's White House staff when he signed the first FISA law, passed overwhelmingly in 1978 with bipartisan support ranging all the way from Strom Thurmond to Ted Kennedy. FISA was Congress's response to Nixon-era abuses, including wiretapping of antiwar activists and political opponents under a broad justification of "national security" (the claim used to justify the coverup of the Watergate burglary, which involved former CIA officers). It was one of several rollbacks of executive branch power during the post-Nixon era that so alarmed Dick Cheney and like-minded Bush officials. Carter did not object to the bill but, like any president, he was not in any hurry to dilute the powers of his office.

The key word in the FISA law was "foreign"—the legislation was designed to regulate surveillance of communications abroad for espionage or war-fighting purposes (NSA's principal mission was to provide "combat support" to the Defense Department). It was a means to ensure the government got the intelligence needed for national security in a way consistent with the Fourth Amendment, which the

Church Committee back in 1975 found had been routinely violated by the CIA, NSA, and J. Edgar Hoover's FBI. The mechanism was a new independent federal court that would review requests to allow the government to listen in on foreign communications (mostly wired telephones, which today we would call landlines). In the decades that followed, the FISA court rarely if ever turned down a warrant request, because warrants were carefully proposed by a Justice Department office and the intelligence committees in the Congress were notified of each one.

As it turned out, the law itself was less an impediment to protecting the country than an excuse for government officials to avoid taking what they saw as unacceptable risks. The Bremer Commission report in July 2000 observed that the FBI was applying FISA in a "cumbersome and overly cautious" manner against terrorism. To obtain a FISA order, the statute required only probable cause—a fairly low legal bar to clear—that the person being surveilled was a member of a terrorist organization. In practice, the Justice Department's Office of Intelligence Policy and Review (OIPR), which processed the surveillance requests, required evidence of wrongdoing or specific knowledge of the group's terrorist intentions in addition to the person's membership in the organization. Also, OIPR did not generally consider the past activities of the surveillance target—such as frequent travel to Afghanistan or pro-terrorist statements on the internet—relevant in determining whether the FISA probable-cause test was met.

We would learn later that FBI agents would not look at

the laptop of Zacarias Moussaoui—one of the original Al
Qaeda militants assigned to be a hijacker on 9/11—because
they feared the legal standard had not been met to justify
a warrant for the search (it did, with room to spare). The
Bremer Commission recommended directing the Department of Justice to enforce the FISA law *as written*, not as
overcautiously interpreted by government attorneys. We argued for a significant expansion of staffing and funding for
OIPR to speed up processing of warrants. We also concluded
that the NSA, the defense agency responsible for technical
collections of information, was "losing its capability to target and exploit the modern communications systems used
by terrorists." The commission recommended that "funding for counterterrorism efforts by CIA, NSA, and FBI must
be given higher priority to ensure continuation of important operational activity and to close the technology gap that
threatens their ability to collect and exploit terrorist communications."

Too often in government a massive failure caused by in-
correct application of existing laws or misuse of existing resources is turned into justification for more legal authority
and more resources. The same held true for the Bush White
House after 9/11. It was clear after the attacks that FISA
needed a reboot to reflect better the realities of modern communications technology and a more diverse and unpredict-
able enemy: nonstate groups and individuals who, like the
9/11 hijackers, may be operating within U.S. territory. As
was noted at the time, with respect to terrorism communications the NSA was looking outside the country and the FBI

was looking inside, but no one was really focused on how to share information between the two.

In the wake of 9/11, Congress on a bipartisan basis was prepared to update outdated laws, albeit with some limits and sunset provisions. But the White House, led by the vice president's office, again chose to develop policies exclusively under the authority granted to the president as commander in chief under Article II of the Constitution. This position was supported by legal opinions provided by the Justice Department that were never shared with Congress. The failure to consult Congress and follow or update existing law caused avoidable problems. Revelations about collecting telephone conversations and email exchanges created a political and media firestorm. The administration was forced to share more information—incomplete and misleading, as it turned out—to justify the program (the full extent of NSA activity post-9/11 would not be known until the Edward Snowden leaks many years later). The surveillance issue—technically complex, legally obscure—did not have the same visceral effect as the detainee treatment controversies discussed earlier: no disturbing photos of abuse splashed across the web or chilling descriptions of captives being tormented. But it is no less important to our identity and values as a free people.

To prevent or disrupt terror plots, early warning and prevention are paramount. For the most part, I supported the goals of the post-9/11 surveillance programs. I did so under the presumption—false, again, as it turns out—that the White House was running these programs lawfully, in a manner consistent with FISA. I would spend much of Bush's second term advocating legislation to put these programs on a solid legal footing consistent with FISA and the Constitution, in particular its Fourth Amendment protections. By the time President Obama took office and began his own robust assertions of executive authority, the Congress was able to establish, however imperfectly, what a legal and politically sustainable framework should look like.

To return to Ben Franklin's formulation: The values of freedom and safety are *not* a zero-sum game, in which one grows at the expense of the other. If done lawfully, liberty (including privacy) and security are mutually reinforcing. As we learned the hard way, before and after 9/11, getting this right is a continuous work in progress as threats to both our liberty—and security—continue to proliferate.

The principal legislative response to the surveillance gaps exposed on 9/11 was the USA PATRIOT Act, passed just weeks after the attacks. It updated a law authorizing collection of traditional telephone calls to apply to internet communications. Back in the 1990s the Clinton administration had begun to work on surveillance legislation to include the internet but ran into stiff resistance on Capitol Hill. Many progressive Democrats and libertarians objected to the enhanced government powers to wiretap, trace email and internet communications, conduct searches, and detain noncitizens. Another criticism was that the PATRIOT Act was rushed, providing little opportunity for members to read and reflect before casting their vote. We knew the bill was far from perfect and contained some potential for overreach. That's why I insisted on sunset provisions that would allow us to fix and tweak the law as circumstances changed.

In those early years, however, the PATRIOT Act—passed by bipartisan majorities, signed by the president—was window dressing. The White House view was that the president had Article II authority to go outside the restraints of FISA if Americans were somehow allegedly involved in a "chain" of phone calls beginning with a "dirty number" connected to a suspected foreign terrorist outside the United States. The program, which was code-named Stellar Wind and required the cooperation of major telecommunications companies, only applied at first to communications involving at least one foreign source. Later the program grew to include collecting, on a massive scale, metadata transmitted within the United States that was connected to suspects overseas. This did not reveal the content of a communication, just its originator, recipient, duration, and, in the case of emails, subject lines. These would all be analyzed by NSA for suspicious patterns, using massive new supercomputers purchased for that purpose. Much of the program was defensible on the grounds that it allowed U.S. intelligence to track the communications and transactions of individuals suspected to have terrorist ties. But safeguards could have been put in place. In my capacity as ranking member on HPSCI, I was a member of the so-called Gang of Eight—a bipartisan group of eight House and Senate leaders who receive briefings on sensitive intelligence matters from the executive branch. I was regularly assured that the program fully complied with the law. Immediately after 9/11 I believed Congress would have updated FISA if asked to do so. In the process the administration would have gained more public trust and acceptance for what followed, instead of a blast of recriminations.

One of the earliest Gang of Eight briefings was held in Vice President Cheney's office on July 17, 2003, four months after the American invasion of Iraq. I was there along with House Intelligence Committee chair Porter Goss and Senators Pat Roberts and John Rockefeller, chair and ranking member of the Senate Intelligence Committee. The briefing was conducted by George Tenet, still CIA director at the time, and General Michael Hayden, the director of NSA. I would later joust with Hayden on the legality of NSA's activities, but I would always admire his formidable intellect and dedication to protecting the country; subsequently we became friends.

During this White House briefing I was assured the program was lawful, though I was not given specifics. I assumed the authority governing the program was FISA. As it turned out, the White House was referring not to FISA but to Justice Department OLC opinions (the same group that provided the "extensive organ failure" standard for defining torture). The fact that FISA was not cited specifically during the briefing should have been a red flag. As with the CIA briefings on enhanced interrogations, I understood that the information was highly classified. Discussing it, or even acknowledging its existence, was a felony offense. To his credit, Senator Rockefeller hand-wrote a brief letter to Cheney to voice concerns about the "profound oversight issues" associated with the NSA collection activities. He also chafed at the classification restrictions that prevented members from consulting with any staff or experts—which turned out to be convenient for the administration.

In response to later criticism, the White House argued against using the FISA court because of the procedural delays. I heard a version of this argument from NSA professionals I greatly respected. But the genius of the American constitutional system is its adaptability. The "captures" provision of Article I, Section 8 may have been written with the Barbary pirates in mind (as discussed earlier), but the same principle applied to Al Qaeda detainees. The Fourth Amendment was a reaction to the opening of mail and ransacking of homes by British officials before the Revolution, but the "right of the people to be secure in their persons, houses, papers, and effects, against unreasonable searches and seizures"—that is, without a warrant informed by probable cause—extended to modern communications as well. This principle is enduring.

The evolution of the PATRIOT Act, which came up for reauthorization in 2005, showed the value of the legislative path not taken. One of the main examples of contention was Section 215, which allowed the government to obtain— with a court order—any records or other "tangible things" under FISA. Because library records were included, among many other sources, Section 215 immediately (and inaccurately) become known as the "library provision," attracting protest from the ACLU and, predictably, the American Library Association. The problem was that terrorists might use the internet at a public library to search for bomb-making instructions or other telltale information. As initially drafted, the law could be construed to enable review of the books someone was reading, which was arguably an overreach. My recommendation was to require that the subject of a Section 215 records search be an "agent of a foreign power," the traditional standard for FISA (Al Qaeda members or affiliates would count as foreign agents). I observed that "without this requirement, Section 215 is open-ended and susceptible to abuse." That summer I co-sponsored a bill with Bernie Sanders (then a House member)—my only legislative collaboration with the independent from Vermont—to remedy some of these provisions.

I recommended other PATRIOT Act reforms, including revising "John Doe" roving wiretaps where neither the identity nor location of the target is known, a situation that could lead to generalized surveillance of all people fitting certain ethnic descriptions. Another PATRIOT Act provision allowed a lower standard of justification than criminal probable cause for domestic intelligence surveillance. I thought the collection should be allowed using the lower standard under some circumstances. But any U.S. citizen targeted by a FISA search that failed to turn up evidence should be informed of the search after a period of time. Despite the fears of early critics, the PATRIOT Act produced a negligible number of documented abuses. One of them entailed an Oregon man named Brandon Mayfield, an American Muslim attorney who was wrongly arrested and imprisoned on suspicion that he was connected to the Madrid train bombings in March 2004. Mayfield was not told that the government conducted secret surveillance on him and his family, though it soon became clear that he was innocent of any terrorist involvement.

The House reauthorized the PATRIOT Act with the reforms I recommended, and other fixes, by an overwhelming bipartisan majority on December 14, 2005. It was a tough vote for me, and I said, "My view of the PATRIOT Act is we need to mend it, not end it. Today we are mending it. Hopefully, soon, we will mend it further." Next was the U.S. Senate, where approval was also expected after a certain amount of debate and pushback. Two days later, however, everything changed.

The *New York Times* headline read: "Bush Altered Rules on Spying in U.S.; He Allowed Warrantless Eavesdropping." The article, based primarily on leaks from a Justice Department official, said that the NSA was recording the calls and emails of up to 500 people in the United States at any given time. The cumulative number of U.S. residents surveilled to that point was somewhere between 5,000 and 7,000. The story made clear that calls and emails made wholly within the U.S. still complied with FISA, but the article did not mention the domestic metadata collection program (described earlier).

The article's publication did not come as a surprise to the Bush administration—or to me. Shortly before the 2004 presidential election the *Times* was all set to run approximately the same story. The White House urged the paper to hold the story, claiming publication would impede efforts to prevent the next major terrorist attack. At that time the members of the Gang of Eight were also enlisted to urge the *Times* not to publish. I was convinced the NSA program was valuable and believed assurances that it was lawful. At the White House's request, I called Phil Taubman, the *Times*' Washington bureau chief, and urged him to hold the story. We would learn later that my call had little impact on the *Times*' decision to withhold the story. But it would become a talking point for critics later.

A few months later, *Times* reporter Eric Lichtblau cornered me after a hearing as I was walking with some of my staff. The 2005 PATRIOT Act reauthorization was then being debated. Lichtblau asked me to square what the administration was saying about privacy protections in the legislation with what his reporting revealed about the NSA surveillance. In effect, Lichtblau was trying to get me to confirm the existence of arguably the most highly classified program in the U.S. government. My staff, who were not cleared for the program, were standing next to us. I was startled and took Lichtblau aside, away from my legislative aides and anyone else who might overhear, and told him that we should not be having such a conversation. He kept pressing for details about the program and its legality. I wouldn't bite, saying only that the program was valuable and the *Times* had made the right decision not to publish (in retrospect, I shouldn't have said even that). The conversation, to the extent there was one, ended abruptly. Knowing the *Times* was getting ready to publish toward the end of the year, the White House made a last-ditch effort to get Congress to intervene to keep the program out of public view. They failed, and the *New York Times* article became an immediate sensation.

The publication of the article—posted online the evening of Friday, December 16—put me in a difficult position. I was barraged by media requests for comment on a program that I was still legally prevented from discussing. The other Democratic HPSCI members, who had not been read in, also had questions. The next day, the Congress was in session as part of the year-end rush. The president declassified much of the program in his Saturday-morning radio address. Sitting in my office, I called Jeff Smith, the former general counsel of the CIA, then working in a D.C. law firm, for some guidance about the program's legality. Jeff said that there was no way it could have been operated under FISA. I was shocked and felt strongly that our committee needed to be briefed. So I called General Hayden, who was now the deputy DNI, on his cell phone. He was out Christmas shopping for his wife at a mall in Maryland. I asked him if he would brief our committee that same afternoon. Hayden said he was available but needed permission from White House chief of staff Andy Card. I reached Card, who first said yes and then called back to say no. It turns out that the White House, which, as I've noted, had plenty of advance warning that a story was coming, was prepping an all-hands effort to push back at the *Times*. As far I was concerned the president's partial declassifying of the program meant my HPSCI colleagues should get the same information that I had. My frustration came through in a statement issued a few days later:

> As the Ranking Democrat on the House Intelligence Committee, I have been briefed since 2003 on a highly classified NSA foreign collection program that targeted Al Qaeda. I believe the program is essential to US national security and that its disclosure has damaged critical intelligence capabilities. . . . Like many Americans, I am deeply concerned by reports that this program in fact goes far beyond the measures to target Al Qaeda about which I was briefed.

The days before Christmas, usually a time when D.C. shuts down, instead were consumed by furious Democratic—and some Republican—criticisms of the program and an equally determined White House counteroffensive. I joined a letter signed by all HPSCI Democrats asking for a classified briefing followed by open and closed hearings as soon as Congress reconvened in January. While the White House continued to assert that the program was focused on foreign terrorism-related communications, it was becoming clear that a good deal of domestic traffic was being scooped up as well. In a statement on December 21, I reiterated my position: "Domestic-to-domestic surveillance requires the approval of a FISA court. It has always been my view that the President must seek FISA approval if domestic-to-domestic surveillance is involved." In emergency situations FISA allowed for a seventy-two-hour waiting period for surveillance to take place while the warrant was getting approved. My statement concluded: "Once armed with full information, Congress can and should change the laws regarding domestic surveillance if warranted."

In his radio address following the December *New York Times* story, Bush said that he had authorized NSA "to intercept the international communications of people with known links to al Qaeda and related terrorist organizations. Before we intercept these communications, the government must have information that establishes a clear link to these terrorist networks." The White House later rebranded the overall NSA effort—known internally as the President's Surveillance Program—as the Terrorist Surveillance Program (TSP) for public consumption. That also allowed the administration to be narrowly—if misleadingly—accurate in its public statements. The warrantless surveillance of communications activity defended by the White House under the TSP moniker did have some connection to terrorism. The TSP notably did not include the broader and more indiscriminate Stellar Wind effort, which had not yet been divulged.

Members of Congress were having none of it. On December 23, Tom Daschle, who was Senate majority leader during the events of 9/11, responded: "I can state categorically that the subject of warrantless wiretaps of American citizens never came up. I did not and never would have supported giving authority to the president for such wiretaps." Daschle then revealed that on the evening of September 12,

2001, the White House had proposed that Congress authorize the use of military force to "deter and pre-empt any future acts of terrorism *or aggression* against the United States." This broad mandate could include actions that had nothing to do with 9/11, Al Qaeda, or even necessarily terrorism. Congressional leaders at the time pushed back and settled with the administration on different language: "all necessary and appropriate force against those nations, organizations or persons [the president] determines planned, authorized, committed or aided" the attacks of September 11. The authority was still expansive—but at least it was tied to the terror attacks that had spawned the resolution in the first place. Then, at the last minute—literally, according to Daschle—the White House sought to add the words "in the United States" after "appropriate force." Those words would extend the president's powers as commander in chief to cover American citizens and legal residents. They would provide a fig leaf of legal cover for the domestic surveillance program.

After the Bush announcement the administration turned to General Hayden and its attorney general, Alberto Gonzales, to tell its story to the press and on the Hill. Gonzales's legal justification was that surveillance of enemy communications was a standard wartime tool permitted under the AUMF resolution, which took precedence over FISA. Even without the AUMF, the president had the authority under Article II to do what he wanted during a time of war. These points were reinforced in a forty-two-page white paper released by the attorney general that was designed to head off demands by many in the Congress and news media for copies of the original Justice Department OLC memos. That same kind of legal reasoning had blown up in the administration's face with respect to detainees. But the White House pressed on.

On February 1, I wrote to the president that "the activities of the NSA program can—and should—be accomplished within the law, not by circumventing it." I pointed out that the PATRIOT Act and FISA reauthorization "had sought—and Congress approved—numerous changes to FISA to reflect the fact that terrorists use multiple cell phones, e-mail accounts, and the Internet." For example, prior to the PATRIOT Act, the government could obtain a FISA order for "pen-register" (recording the telephone numbers of outgoing calls) and "trap and trace" (incoming calls) only upon certifying that the phone line was or would be used by a suspected spy or terrorist. Under the PATRIOT Act, such an order could be obtained "for any investigation to gather foreign intelligence information" that the government certified as "relevant." This lower standard also applied to email and internet traffic. I cited several other instances in which Congress had adapted FISA after 9/11 to give the government more tools and flexibility. Indeed, even though I was one of a handful of members who were briefed on the NSA surveillance, it was not clear to me why FISA could not cover the entire program: "If the post-9/11 amendments are insufficient, why were they proposed? If the modifications made by the PATRIOT Act are still inadequate, why didn't the Administration propose additional changes?"

HPSCI finally got at least some of the information we had been calling for when Hayden and Gonzales briefed us for four hours in closed session. Originally they were only going to discuss the program's legal rationale but, facing pushback from Hoekstra and me, they broadened the scope to include some operational aspects as well. I told reporters afterward that with this thawing in the White House hard line "the ice is falling." It was a start, but not enough. I was encouraged that one of my Republican colleagues—Heather Wilson, a brilliant Rhodes Scholar and former air force officer (later secretary of the air force)—asked for a full congressional inquiry. Wilson would go on to draft legislation to bring more of the surveillance program under FISA. Congress was at least stepping up to some of its Article I responsibilities.

Around this time Cheney told Fox News that Congress had no business complaining now because its top leaders, including Democrats such as Pelosi and me, had been briefed fully. In a February appearance on *Meet the Press*, I replied: "The briefings were about the operational details of the program. I support the program. I've never flinched from that. However, the briefings were not about the legal underpinnings of the program." When pressed on why I hadn't inquired or objected immediately after the briefings, I explained: "I talked to absolutely no one, because I would have violated three different federal criminal statutes had I talked to anybody." I pointed out again that, according to the 1947 National Security Act, the Gang of Eight process was supposed to be limited to the most sensitive covert *action* programs. The NSA surveillance "is not a covert action program . . . [it]

is a very valuable foreign collection program." Expanding the briefings to all HPSCI members, Cheney had argued, would lead to leaks. I pointed out that disclosures to the *New York Times* had come from the executive branch, not the Congress.

The rest of 2006 would be consumed by a legislative battle to bring the NSA program under U.S. law. As with detainee policy, the White House and most Republicans pushed bills that basically would have given congressional imprimatur to everything being done already—and, in some cases, authorizing more. That wasn't going to cut it for me. In fact, on April 26, for the first time in my congressional career, I voted against an intelligence authorization bill to protest the administration's law-free surveillance programs. I was incensed that the Republican-led House Rules Committee, the institutional gatekeeper for any legislation, rejected a bipartisan bill I had co-sponsored that should have been a no-brainer. It clarified that all surveillance of Americans on U.S. soil must follow the law and Constitution. The other sponsors included California Democrat Adam Schiff and Arizona Republican Jeff Flake, both of whom would gain more prominence later during the Trump administration.

The revelations also raised new questions about government secrecy and press freedoms. While I opposed the *New York Times*' publication of the NSA story, I was also troubled that Attorney General Gonzales suggested journalists could be prosecuted for printing national security–related information. In an ongoing case, the Justice Department took the position that the oral receipt of information and the retransmission of that information constitutes a violation of the Espionage Act. In an April 26 HPSCI hearing I pointed out that the theory, "if true[,] would punish not just every reporter for the *Los Angeles Times*, but every reader of the newspaper who discusses what they read with their neighbors."

As a general proposition, I applauded my Republican colleagues—Arlen Specter in the Senate, Heather Wilson in the House—who were trying to put a legal framework around the surveillance. The problem, from the perspective of someone who had been read in to the NSA program, is that "these bills are solutions in search of a problem," as I said in a statement issued in July. In effect, they would create new sources of authority even though the desired surveillance could (and should) be done completely under the existing FISA system. And the Specter and Wilson bills would have provided a blanket authorization for domestic surveillance, which is not consistent with the Fourth Amendment.

Later that spring I introduced (along with John Conyers, ranking member of the House Judiciary Committee) the LISTEN Act, which stated that the 2001 AUMF did not allow electronic surveillance outside FISA. It was endorsed by the ACLU, the American Bar Association, and other civil liberties organizations. Other legislation was being drafted as well, in some cases by Republicans who had not been read in to the program and were presuming that the existing FISA law was more restrictive of necessary surveillance than was actually the case. The administration stoked that impression when General Keith Alexander, the current NSA director, argued that there were simply too many calls and emails to get FISA warrants for all of them. Knowing what I did about the program, I knew that the numbers were manageable, and I was convinced that the overarching principle was non-negotiable.

In a July HPSCI hearing I said: "As someone briefed on the NSA program, I have seen no reason why we should change the requirement for individualized warrants. If the government needs more resources to obtain warrants in an emergency, the LISTEN Act provides those resources." I pointed out to Hoekstra that under Wilson's bill, "you could be on Committee business abroad and decide to call your wife in Michigan . . . and the government would not need a warrant to listen in. That is a slippery slope."

When I became the chair of the Homeland Security Sub-committee on Intelligence, Information Sharing, and Terrorism Risk Assessment in 2007, I continued to be active in the legislative battle over FISA. Under intense White House pressure, enough Democrats voted with Republicans to pass the Protect America Act (PAA) in August 2007. Along the lines of Republican legislation debated the previous year, the PAA provided statutory cover for most of the existing surveillance program. I ultimately could not support the final version of the PAA because it did not provide adequate privacy safeguards. In casting my vote I noted that it was a short-term law, due to expire in February 2008, and urged the Congress to begin working on a more balanced (and constitutional) framework to replace it.

In his January 28, 2008, State of the Union address President Bush had pressured Congress for an immediate extension and, turning to a familiar line of rhetoric, warned that if it was not granted, "our ability to track terrorist threats would be weakened and our citizens could be in greater danger." My response: "It is inaccurate and, yet again, a bald-faced attempt to play the fear card and jam Congress into gutting a carefully crafted, three-decades-old bipartisan law." I pointed out that FISA, which enabled lawful surveillance, was not expiring—only the hastily cobbled-together Protect America Act amendments were. "This country will not go dark . . . our government has aggressively used surveillance tools and, in the past year or so, secured warrants in compliance with FISA."

The White House continued to warn of possible terror attacks as a means to bring vulnerable Democrats into line, but DNI and CIA threat briefings to the Congress contained no new information. The Senate, on a bipartisan basis, approved a surveillance bill that I still considered unacceptable. My message to the intelligence community: "We need to conduct surveillance of foreign terrorists, but we must do it within the rule of law. With a clear legal framework, you are empowered to do your job better—and from that we all benefit."

After the Israelis killed a senior Hezbollah leader in February 2008, the administration again claimed an immediate reauthorization of the Protect America Act was needed to protect against possible reprisals against the United States. I was disappointed to see that DNI Mike McConnell made public statements closely echoing White House talking points. The prior September McConnell had been forced to retract testimony claiming that the new Protect America Act (passed in August) had played a role in helping to thwart a terrorist plot: earlier that month, German authorities, acting on U.S. intelligence, had arrested three men on suspicion of plotting car bombings that could have killed many Americans in Europe. The problem was that the U.S. intercepts warning of the plot had been given to the Germans more than a year prior, before the Protect America Act passed.

One of the other sticking points was the use—and, in some cases, abuse—of national security letters, documents issued by the FBI in advance of investigating particular individuals deemed worrisome from a security perspective but without probable cause of a crime. Too often these were used to provide a blank check to access otherwise constitutionally protected personal information. In February I introduced the National Security Letter Judicial and Congressional Oversight Act, requiring a FISA court judge or designated U.S. federal magistrate to approve the issuance of such a letter. The FBI inspector general later revealed that the Bureau had overreached in using national security letters. This legislation would clarify the government's authority and its limits. My relationship with the ACLU had its ups and downs over the years (from my perspective, their absolutist positions sometimes did not take security concerns seriously enough), but they strongly applauded the national security letters bill and, for a very short time, me as well.

These efforts paid off in July 2008 with compromise FISA legislation I could support. On the House floor I said:

> My phones are ringing off the hook and my email accounts are full. By the hundreds, and hundreds, my constituents are saying "don't cave in," "don't toss due process out the window," "no compromise on our civil liberties" and "all surveillance of Americans should require a warrant." One of the most powerful messages said: "The U.S. Constitution has been 'marked up.' Don't shred it."

The compromise replaced bad law (the Protect America Act) with a FISA bill that made clear that "no President can ignore it, ever again. . . . In short: no more warrantless surveillance." It also expanded the circumstances for which individual warrants were required by including Americans outside the United States (previous versions had simply allowed the NSA to surveil Americans overseas without a warrant for virtually any reason). It required federal court review to determine whether the telecommunications firms that assisted the post-9/11 surveillance would get civil liability protection, contrary to oft-repeated claims that the firms were automatically immunized.

A supporter of FISA compromise was Senator Barack Obama. Some claimed Obama, then about to secure the Democratic Party nomination for president, voted for the bill to shore up his national security credentials in advance of the general election. It's telling, however, that the surveillance provisions of the 2008 FISA law signed by Bush 43 survived with only minor tweaks through congressional reauthorizations during the Obama administration. Years later I remain convinced that the Congress finally came together to get it right. The 2008 FISA bill was one of the last truly bipartisan pieces of major legislation to be passed before obstruction and gridlock became the norm.

Obama left much of the NSA operation intact. A certain part of the electorate never accepted the need for robust surveillance under any circumstance. Younger Americans without vivid memories of the 9/11 attacks were less inclined to trust their government—or established institutions generally—in the wake of the Iraq debacle and the 2008 financial crisis. One of those, an NSA contractor named Edward Snowden, took it upon himself in the summer of 2013 to show the world the inner workings and structure of America's national security surveillance operation.

Some considered Snowden a whistleblower hero in the tradition of Daniel Ellsberg, who leaked the Pentagon Papers documenting government deceptions during the Vietnam War. As I told *PBS NewsHour* shortly afterward: "He's a leaker. And what he did was inappropriate." I pointed out that all the NSA programs were under the jurisdiction of the FISA court. Oversight was provided by the intelligence committees—then ably led by Dianne Feinstein and Richard Burr in the Senate and Mike Rogers and Dutch Ruppersberger in the House. And I explained about the data being collected: "This is metadata. It's telephone numbers, not attached to people. And the only access you can get to this metadata, if a U.S. citizen or a U.S. legal resident is involved, is on an individual basis once you go through a federal court to get an individualized warrant, which is what the Fourth Amendment requires."

The harm the leak caused to America's national security and international relationships was profound. Our surveillance tool box was exposed. Anti-American sentiment peaked in Germany over the news that the United States had eavesdropped on the country's chancellor, Angela Merkel. Part of the collateral damage—not a national security calamity, but still telling—was Brazil's rejection of an American company's bid on a multibillion-dollar fighter jet contract due to the Snowden revelations.

By 2020 the *New York Times* was reporting that the NSA stopped the metadata collection because it found that the program simply hadn't produced useful information. According to a declassified internal study, NSA had spent $100 million over the prior four years analyzing the logs of domestic phone calls. The result was a total of two unique leads and one significant investigation. In hindsight it is clear that rapidly evolving technology will outgrow any legal framework. That is why laws on government surveillance need vigorous oversight and sunset clauses. If a program isn't working, it should be ended. Arguably there is a greater national security risk from continuing to prop up—out of bureaucratic pride or habit—

collection tools that may no longer be effective (or, in some cases, were never really effective to begin with). In retrospect it's remarkable to think how much time and energy were expended briefing and later debating an NSA phone metadata program that turned out to have marginal utility at best.

Meanwhile, the proverbial battlefield has shifted. We have been very successful at taking out the physical infrastructure of terrorism, so groups have been forced to migrate online for recruiting, organizing, and planning. At the same time, social media is now a universal phenomenon. Huge internet companies—Facebook, Twitter, and others—routinely collect quantities of personal information (browsing habits, shopping choices, reading preferences) that the NSA could only dream of. Mark Zuckerberg expressed shock at the Snowden revelations, yet he runs a company whose business model is based on exploiting the multiple petabytes' worth of data it collects about its billion-plus active users monthly. To satisfy a global customer base with strict privacy expectations, Silicon Valley has developed technical capabilities to put customer data under lock and key. Apple famously continues to deny FBI requests to provide access to the smartphone data of even the most dangerous criminal suspects.

The effectiveness of mass government surveillance and data collection grows more limited each day. Would-be terrorists now become radicalized and spread their message over social networks under private corporate control: Facebook, YouTube, and others. Importantly, these commercial companies are *not* held to the same Fourth Amendment and other privacy protections as the U.S. government. Arguably

the most effective method for detecting extremists—
international or domestic—lies not in mass data collection
but through the monitoring of social media by individuals
trained to recognize potentially dangerous exchanges. In
many respects, the human factor has become more important, not less. The technology has changed, but the game
hasn't. Artificial intelligence may one day perform most of
this function, but there is no avoiding the requirement for
people to be involved in monitoring much of the content.
Chastened and on the political defensive, Silicon Valley ap-
pears willing to be more public-minded about the content
hosted on their servers. The operative law remains the 1996
Communications Decency Act, which prevents holding social media companies accountable on their platforms. A
fierce assault by the Trump administration failed, but there
remains substantial bipartisan political support to change
the law.

The politics of surveillance have shifted from the bipartisan
consensus and resulting legal framework established more
than a decade ago. The far left is hostile to most national
security functions of government, especially when privacy is
involved. The right has become newly appreciative of civil
liberties after the investigative and prosecutorial powers of
the federal government were turned on several of Trump's
associates after the 2016 election. I never bought the con-
spiracy theories about the "deep state." But as someone who
has gone through the experience of being wiretapped and

then having selective information leaked to the press, I appreciated the concern (if not the partisan motivation). The Justice Department's own inspector general's report found that the original FISA request to surveil a Trump campaign aide (Carter Page) was lawful but the follow-up applications (after the election) were not. That's an argument for tightening standards and oversight, not for dispensing with the law and surveillance capabilities altogether.

Unfortunately, it was in this hothouse political climate that Congress took up extending several FISA provisions due to expire in mid-March 2020. In a rare recent example of bipartisan legislating, the House leadership agreed to extend the provisions while making reforms to protect privacy. For example, the House bill would push the FISA court to appoint an outside ombudsperson for wiretap applications involving sensitive First Amendment activity, including political campaigns. Additionally, the government could not use an order for business records (permitted under FISA for national security investigations) to collect information that would otherwise require a criminal search warrant, such as cell phone location data. The Senate, under pressure from activists unsatisfied with the new House protections, passed a temporary extension of the three surveillance tools with the intent of negotiating a fuller package later.

President Trump, still bitter about what he considered a "witch hunt" by the FBI, tweeted that he was inclined to veto the reauthorization of FISA unless major changes were made—and perhaps not even then. As it turned out, Trump never was forced to make that veto—the House adjourned for spring break in 2020 without voting on the temporary FISA extension already passed by the Senate. Because the expiration did not impact ongoing investigations (though it may complicate starting new ones), the Congress did not feel a great sense of urgency. So after a promising bipartisan start, the Congress punted again on its Article I responsibilities, not unlike its inaction on a new AUMF.

Regardless of who is doing the surveilling, we continue to face a textbook dilemma: a choice between two undesirable options. Should government limit its own ability to track bad behavior, even if such tracking could possibly save lives—say, by identifying COVID-19 carriers, or by responding to the online ravings of potential mass shooters? Or should citizens be willing to relinquish some freedom and privacy in exchange for more safety—something Ben Franklin warned against? Even in the name of gaining more security, few Americans could countenance the route taken by China, where sophisticated facial recognition and artificial intelligence enable tracking on a massive scale. The dystopian scenario portrayed in the BBC/Netflix series *Black Mirror*, in which everyone's digital social score is being continuously upgraded or downgraded based on daily interactions, is close to reality in China, with its "social credit" system.

I dealt with these kinds of questions in the Congress when passing legislation in 2007 to explore, and ultimately sever, the connection between extremist views and terrorist acts— later distorted by critics into a "thought crimes" bill. Does reciting online parts of the Quran that incite violence justify scrutiny or intervention, whether it's by the state or delegated to the tech providers? Should irresponsible behavior, such as violating a COVID-19 restriction by going to a bar with friends, also be monitored and policed? Hypothetical scenarios such as these are why any potential legislation should be preceded by a national conversation—similar to what occurred before Congress took up the Anti-Ballistic Missile treaty, authorizing and funding MX missiles during the 1980s, or during investigations of past intelligence abuses, as with the Church Commission in the 1970s. Congress still has the power to convene experts and set a national agenda. It is imperative that America's collection tools and laws match the threats and technologies of our time. The alternative is living under an increasingly indiscriminate surveillance system that would neither protect liberty nor provide security.

SIX

Presidential Power
Unchecked and Unbalanced

On March 15, 2006, the newly elected president of Liberia, Ellen Johnson Sirleaf, was at the Capitol to address a joint session of Congress. Dick Cheney would be up there as well, sitting behind the Liberian president, along with the Speaker of the House. After the speech the vice president went to his ornate office near the Senate chamber. Cheney considered himself a part of the legislative branch as well as the executive branch because the Constitution assigned the vice president to cast a tiebreaking vote in the Senate. Nonetheless, Cheney didn't spend much time on the Hill. One of many mysteries about Cheney is how someone who had risen to House minority whip while a congressman from Wyoming could become so contemptuous of the institution he once helped lead.

I first met Cheney at a Renaissance Weekend winter retreat in 1992 soon after I was first elected. He had just finished nearly four years as a highly regarded secretary of defense. He had overseen the U.S. military response to the Iraqi invasion of Kuwait while keeping the firm hand of civilian control on the Pentagon's top brass. At the Renaissance Weekend he was congenial and gracious, telling me that I was going to "love" being in the Congress. Cheney was a far cry from the obsessive, almost maniacal figure he would be portrayed as during his terms as vice president. He later claimed that he hadn't changed; the world had—after 9/11.

Fast-forward to 2006. As HPSCI ranking member, I had for weeks been pleading with the White House to expand classified briefings on the Stellar Wind surveillance program to the full committee. I heard Cheney was going to be in his Senate office after he presided at the Sirleaf Johnson speech, so I took the opportunity to talk with him in person. After the usual pleasantries, I got right to it. "Mr. Vice President," I said, "there's a lot of concern in the House about Stellar Wind. Please allow more than two people to be briefed on it." Cheney leaned forward, adopting that trademark sphinx position of his. With his face impassive, his eyes staring right at me, he said, "No." That was it. End of conversation.

I was frustrated. My short stint as special counsel to DoD in the early 1980s and my service on HASC and HPSCI made it clear to me that Cheney's position was unreasonable. I was a trained lawyer—one of 28 women (out of 550 students) who would graduate from Harvard Law School in 1969, during the height of the Vietnam War (also a product of presidential hubris). At law school, I gravitated toward international law—and became research assistant to Professor Abram Chayes, who had been legal advisor to the State Department during the Kennedy years. Chayes was a proponent of using force when necessary but only when it was matched with patient diplomacy and consistent with international law. Chayes was involved in Robert Kennedy's 1968 campaign for president, which I was about to join when RFK was assassinated. At Chayes's encouragement—insistence, really—I interviewed for a job at the State Department after graduation. The interviewer: a charming Harvard Law grad eight years my senior who would become my first husband. Chayes passed away in April 2000—a huge loss, as America desperately needed someone like him to guide us through the post-9/11 legal morass. One of his favorite sayings, which has always stayed with me, is: "There's nothing wrong with a lawyer holding the United States to its own best standards and principles."

Among the many landmark Supreme Court cases I'd studied during my years at Harvard Law was *Youngstown Sheet & Tube v. Sawyer*, decided in 1952. What *Brown v. Board of Education* is to desegregation or *Roe v. Wade* is to abortion, the *Youngstown* ruling is to presidential power. In the middle of the Korean War, President Harry Truman seized control of the nation's steel mills before the steelworkers union could go on strike. His legal rationale was that disrupting production would damage the country's ability to wage war, which fell under a president's Article II powers. The steel companies sued, and the Supreme Court ruled that Truman's actions exceeded his constitutional and statutory authorities.

In his concurring opinion, Justice Robert Jackson laid out a framework that has become the standard for bounding presidential executive authority ever since. The president's power is at its "lowest ebb," Jackson held, when the president acts in defiance of Congress's express will. Executive power is at its maximum when the president acts with congressional approval. In between these poles is what Jackson called "the zone of twilight," when the president acts in the absence of congressional direction. The president typically may act, but only as long as Congress does not disagree. Jackson wrote: "With all its defects, delays and inconveniences, men have discovered no technique for long preserving free government except that the Executive be under the law, and that the law be made by parliamentary deliberations."

After law school I joined the staff of California Democratic senator John Tunney, and, with the Watergate scandal, would confront a presidency operating without regard to these zones—or any other restraints. Many people today forget that Watergate, though associated with Nixon's determination to win the 1972 presidential election, had its origins in the president's unilateral pursuit of military action. The first illegal wiretaps, which would later grow into a wide-ranging "plumbers" operation, were intended to stop leaks to the press about the secret bombing of Cambodia, where hundreds of thousands of tons of munitions were dropped without the knowledge of either the Congress or the public. I attended a secret meeting in 1973, roughly two weeks after my oldest son was born. Tunney, Ted Kennedy, and other Democrats on the Senate Judiciary Committee invited one aide each (I was the only woman) to discuss how to respond to the October 20 "Saturday Night Massacre," when President Nixon directed first his attorney general, Elliot Richardson, and then his deputy attorney general, William Ruckelshaus, to fire special prosecutor Archibald Cox; both resigned rather than carry out his order. At the time, the country seemed to be coming apart, and I expected gunfire in the streets. Yet America's constitutional system proved resilient once more, even in the face of repeated challenges and abuses.

After Watergate, I became chief counsel and staff director for the Senate Judiciary Committee's Subcommittee on Constitutional Rights. I vividly recall one episode in which Tunney (who had succeeded Sam Ervin as chair) and I went over to the Supreme Court to meet Chief Justice Warren Burger. We were ushered into room after room until we arrived in the inner sanctum where Burger was standing. He said hello to Tunney. Then he saw me, and his mouth fell open. "When you said you were bringing your chief counsel, I expected someone . . . bigger." It seemed clear that Burger was surprised to see a female lawyer in a leadership role.

Later I would serve in Jimmy Carter's White House as deputy cabinet secretary, writing minutes for cabinet meetings in which the crises of the era were debated, from gas shortages to the Panama Canal. Something I'd learned during that time that has stayed with me ever since was that the White House had no monopoly on wisdom. Perhaps impudently for someone in her early thirties, I aspired to be assistant attorney general in the Justice Department. But Carter's attorney general, Griffin Bell, was known to not have much use for women, even though he was part of a supposedly liberal-minded Democratic administration. After leaving government in 1980, practicing law held little appeal.

I was passionate about public service, so as the Reagan–Bush era wound down, I waited—and hoped—for a congressional seat to open up in Southern California.

Some arrogation of executive authority was inevitable after 9/11—and appropriately so. At a time of war or national crisis, the president's powers as commander in chief are at their zenith constitutionally, as a matter of necessity. Abraham Lincoln suspended habeas corpus during the Civil War. Franklin D. Roosevelt, revered by my family when I was growing up, interned American citizens of Japanese descent after Pearl Harbor. (Lincoln's action held up under historical scrutiny; Roosevelt's has not.) FDR's attorney general, Francis Biddle, who oversaw the detention, wrote: "The Constitution never really bothered a wartime president." Whatever the historical merits or demerits of these assertions of presidential power, they were spurred by a conventional war of finite duration. The executive aggrandizement ended, for the most part, when the wars did. But the open-ended Cold War, with the threat of immediate nuclear conflict, provided excuses to enhance the powers (and secrecy) of the presidency. In each case—from Truman's nationalizing the steel industry to Nixon's cover-up of the Watergate break-in—the Supreme Court or Congress reestablished the constitutional balance.

At least that was the mainstream view. But to a small group of ideological conservatives, the U.S. system had become

dangerously tilted *against* the presidency. Particularly griev-
ous to this group was the collapse of South Vietnam after
Nixon's resignation, when Congress refused to provide military assistance requested by a much-weakened President
Ford. (Ford's chief and deputy chief of staff at the time were,
respectively, Donald Rumsfeld and Dick Cheney.) After
several meetings with Cheney and his underlings I told the
New Yorker: "They've persuaded themselves that, following
Nixon, things went all wrong."

Most of the Congress and public were outraged during
the late 1980s when the Reagan White House diverted funds
from Iranian arms sales to the Nicaraguan Contras. Not only
was it trading money for hostages, it was a blatant violation of
a U.S. law banning assistance to the Central American rebels.
But to Dick Cheney, who was then House minority whip,
the greater outrage was not the diversion of funds but the existence of the Boland Amendment, which barred the military
assistance. Cheney thought Congress had no business telling
the president how to conduct foreign policy—period. With
the Iran-Contra scandal the executive was at the "low ebb"
of authority, according to *Youngstown*, because it had acted
against the explicit direction of Congress. Still, Cheney's
views were documented in a lengthy "minority report" that
was part of the larger report produced by the congressional
committees investigating the Iran-Contra affair. That minority report concluded: "Congressional actions to limit the
president in this area therefore should be reviewed with a con-
siderable degree of skepticism. If they interfere with the core
presidential foreign policy functions, they should be struck

down." The report received little attention at the time, but it served as a manifesto for many who would populate the top ranks of government during the Bush administration. The dominant figure in this group was David Addington, who later served as Cheney's aide and general counsel at DoD, and ultimately became his top lawyer and his second chief of staff as vice president. As far as Addington was concerned, when Article II said that "the executive Power shall be vested in a President," well, that was the end of it—all power, not some power or whatever power Congress provided or allowed. The concept of the "unitary executive," once an obscure theory at the right fringe of legal thinking, would become the operating manual for the Bush presidency when it came to security policy. I called this a "bloodless coup"—a dramatic power shift in government that occurred almost entirely out of view at the time. Addington was always courtly and polite with me personally. But when it came to any role for Congress, his answer was always a very firm no.

Invariably, this view of presidential authority was accompanied by excessive secrecy. The early sign of this tendency, months before 9/11, was Cheney's Energy Task Force. It held a series of meetings—usually with conservative policy analysts or energy company executives—without any public disclosure of the attendees or content, in contravention of the Public Meetings Act. The justification was that disclosures would limit the president's room to gather information and deliberate before making executive decisions—which were ostensibly covered by Article II. The news media and most Democrats protested, but to little avail. (A 2005 appeals court ruling allowed the records of task force meetings to remain secret, and apart from some media disclosures, most of its activities remain unknown even today.) As a legislator and citizen, I found this precedent ominous. If the White House took this position on energy, a domestic policy matter, what claims would be made when it came to national security, where presidents have traditionally asserted the most power?

To Cheney, Addington, and their followers in the Pentagon and Justice Department, the main reason the events of 9/11 had not been prevented was not poorly coordinated intelligence, FBI lassitude, or White House apathy—it was a weakened executive branch. To them, the problem was an NSA unable to do all the needed eavesdropping and a CIA unable (and unwilling) to conduct harsh interrogations and recruit terrorist informants for fear of congressional sanction. 9/11 was considered a political asset to the president— indeed, the centerpiece of his reelection campaign, even as the situation in Iraq was sliding from bad to worse. To be fair, in the weeks and months after 9/11 many of us expected a follow-on attack, and the White House wanted to be able to claim it had done *everything* possible to prevent it. If Democrats and other critics stood in their way, raising concerns about civil liberties and the Geneva Conventions, they could unfairly be portrayed as soft and complicit.

The Bush administration repeatedly asserted that the president's authority as commander in chief either trumped federal statutes or, more often, gave the White House power to interpret laws in a way that provided executive latitude never intended by the Congress. Cheney and his team, then

Bush himself, were not just looking to act without Congress for themselves; they wanted to create precedents for future presidents as well. Years later, after another disclosure of extralegal interrogation memos, I said: "This is a concept of executive authority that was discarded at Runnymede [with the adoption of the Magna Carta] in the thirteenth century and has absolutely no place in our constitutional system."

One of the least known yet most consequential documents filed immediately after 9/11 was a memorandum of notification to Congress, commonly referred to as a "finding," which announced that the CIA would be conducting operations that would not be acknowledged. At the time, this notification, submitted on September 17, 2001, seemed pro forma; we all took it as a given that aggressive covert activity would—indeed, must—be part of our response to the horrific attacks. Yet this same finding would cover the CIA black sites, enhanced interrogations, and targeted killings abroad for nearly two decades.

Congress would ultimately vote on an AUMF for Iraq. The problem with Iraq was not the absence of Congress from the process. It was that our consultation and participation were only as good as the information we received. The intelligence committees were completely dependent on whatever the administration provided, primarily the National Intelligence Estimate. Even those who voted against the Iraq War—for very sound reasons, as it turned out—did so assuming the CIA estimates were mainly correct. The vague and selective briefings, many of which I received as HPSCI ranking member, would continue on surveillance, interrogations, and more. Only press disclosures would eventually force the administration to provide enough information, however grudgingly, for the Congress and the public to make informed decisions and pursue legislative remedies.

The "unitary executive" mindset was spelled out most explicitly in statements appended to legislation that contained provisions the president didn't like but was compelled to sign—bills that had passed with veto-proof majorities, such as the Detainee Treatment Act or funding for the military. The Bush White House made an art form out of these signing statements, claiming authority to ignore certain provisions of more than 120 bills during his presidency—covering everything from fisheries to the Export-Import Bank. The most contentious dealt with national security–related matters—on torture especially. This conflicted directly with the president's constitutional responsibility to "take care that the laws be faithfully executed"—not just the parts of the laws he agreed with. It was turning the *Youngstown* framework on its head.

The modern practice of presidential signing statements had begun under Ronald Reagan, then continued under Bush 41 and Clinton. What set Bush 43 apart was not so much the number of statements but the percentage containing specific constitutional objections—nearly 90 percent by September 2006, according to the Congressional Research Service (the comparable Reagan number was 26 percent). The Bush signing statements flew mostly under the radar at first, until Congress started to pay closer attention. Then the media began to cover the statements as news events in and of themselves. Despite the growing criticism—including from

Republican institutionalists in the Congress—and plummet-
ing political popularity, the Bush White House plowed ahead
undeterred. As late as the fiscal year 2007 defense budget,
Bush issued a signing statement objecting to sixteen provisions (this when the Republicans still controlled the Congress, at least for a few more weeks). For example, the defense
bill barred the Pentagon from using any intelligence that was
collected illegally, including information about Americans
that was gathered in violation of the Fourth Amendment's
protections against unreasonable government surveillance.
Bush's signing statement suggested that the president alone
could decide whether the Pentagon could use such information. Bush also challenged three sections that required
the Pentagon to notify Congress before diverting funds to
new purposes, including top-secret activities or programs
that Congress had already decided against funding. Bush's
statement said he was not bound to obey such statutes if he
decided, as commander in chief, that withholding such information from the Congress was necessary to protect national
security–related secrets. For most of this period the White
House staff secretary coordinating the signing statements was
Brett Kavanaugh, later nominated by President Trump to the
Supreme Court.

Barack Obama famously was the first constitutional law professor to become president (he had been a visiting lecturer
at the University of Chicago). In keeping with a campaign
of "hope and change," he pledged to overturn the excessive

secrecy and aggressive executive claims of the previous administration. During his first year he declassified the Bush Justice Department "torture memos," an action I applauded. Obama would shed welcome daylight on the discredited practices of his predecessor. Yet he was loath to relinquish the presidential authority and secrecy that would prove so useful, and tempting to use, in the wider fight against Al Qaeda.

Obama had virtually no foreign policy experience before being elected to the White House. His credibility on national security—key to his primary victory against Hillary Clinton—stemmed mainly from his opposition to the war in Iraq when he was an Illinois state senator. Obama was going to turn the page not so much on the Bush-Cheney era as on the Democratic establishment, embodied by the Clintons and others who had initially supported the Iraq War (like me). Obama increasingly bypassed Capitol Hill on a range of matters. Not so much for ideological reasons, like the Bush White House, but because he deemed it not particularly useful (or, for that matter, enjoyable). Rounds of golf that could have been spent cultivating elected officials in both parties instead were played mostly with old chums from Hawaii and Chicago. Over time, the two ends of Pennsylvania Avenue grew further and further apart.

The precious two years in which Obama had sizable Democratic majorities—including a nearly filibuster-proof Senate—were consumed almost completely by the construction and passage of the Affordable Care Act (ACA).

It was a great legislative accomplishment, one that I supported, but its political legitimacy and staying power were undermined when it passed without a single Republican vote. The ACA had a huge political cost, as the GOP, running heavily against "Obamacare," seized the House in the next midterm election. After the election, there were few moderate Republicans who would be potential legislative partners. The greater Obama's frustration with recalcitrant Republican majorities—first the Tea Party–dominated House, then the Mitch McConnell–led Senate—the more he would exercise executive action on a range of issues.

Obama acted in the absence of congressional action—in Justice Jackson's "zone of twilight." After repeated congressional rejections of his attempt to close GTMO, even many progressives hoped Obama would simply move the detainees to the United States under his own authority as commander in chief. His former White House counsel, Greg Craig, argued as much toward the end of the administration.

It's telling that the most visible area of overlap between the Bush and Obama administrations' approaches related to the Privacy and Civil Liberties Oversight Board (PCLOB). Created as part of the 2004 intelligence reform legislation, the bipartisan panel was supposed to have five members— four part-time members and one full-time member to serve as chair—cleared to review the most classified counterterror operations for possible civil liberties infractions. With my enthusiastic support, the newly Democratic Congress in 2007 transformed PCLOB into an independent agency within the executive branch and gave it subpoena powers. During his last two years in office Bush declined to put forward a single nominee for the board who had been recommended by Democrats. In return, the Democratic Senate majority refused to confirm Bush's GOP nominees. Two years into the Obama administration, the board was still empty—no one had even been nominated, much less confirmed.

In May 2011, just three months after leaving the Congress, I returned as an outside witness before the Senate Homeland Security and Government Affairs Committee. Reflecting on the successes and shortcomings of the intelligence reform law, I said, "The privacy and civil liberties function is anemic." Without an operational PCLOB, "the U.S. government efforts to improve defenses against critical threats like cyberattack remain opaque and scary. The public doesn't understand why the National Security Agency is in the public sector cyber business, and the Department of Homeland Security hasn't been able to explain its role adequately either. We need public buy-in if these programs are to be successful." Consistent with Ben Franklin's admonition about liberty and safety, a fully functioning PCLOB was necessary not despite a growing domestic terror threat but because of it.

The U.S. government was—and still is—bound by an executive order issued by President Ronald Reagan in 1981 banning the assassination of foreign leaders. Like FISA, Executive Order 12333 was a measure to remedy past abuses. But after the 1983 bombing of the U.S. embassy in Lebanon, the CIA and congressional oversight committees agreed, as reported later in the *Washington Post*, "that if a covert action targeted a terrorist in his apartment plotting to blow up a building, he had to be detained. But if the terrorist were found and known to be on his way to blow up a building . . . he could be killed if that were the only way to stop him." The executive order itself notes that the intelligence community is charged with conducting "special activities" to protect national security, a category under which the drone program falls.

Afghanistan was still very much a war zone in 2011, when I left Congress. With respect to the laws of armed conflict, the drone was simply another weapon of war. The questions at that point were more operational then legal or ethical. The targeting pods and weaponry were not nearly as accurate as equivalent systems today, nor were the underlying intelligence, surveillance, and reconnaissance (ISR) capabilities. Indeed, among the "what-ifs" debated after 9/11 was what might have happened had the Predator drone that tracked Osama Bin Laden's movements in 2000—so that President Clinton could order a cruise missile strike on the Al Qaeda leadership—been armed. In the time it took for the strike to be planned, approved, and launched, Bin Laden and his team had moved (but more than twenty Pakistanis who may or may not have been allied with Al Qaeda were killed). Had the drone been armed, Bin Laden might well have been killed that day instead of surviving to mastermind the 9/11 attacks. Instead, the White House and Pentagon were unwilling to risk either civilian or U.S. casualties in a special operations raid to eliminate Bin Laden the next time he was located. Additionally, Clinton administration lawyers were at loggerheads over whether such a mission was even legal under U.S. law.

Such concerns were far less troubling after 9/11 to the Bush-Cheney White House. From their perspective, this was war, to be fought with all available means—not, as the straw-person argument went, a crime to be prosecuted or a claim to be litigated. No one on the Bush "war council"—the president, vice president, national security advisor, secretary of state, secretary of defense, and their deputies—had been to law school (by contrast, the Clinton and Obama administrations at times felt like an American Bar Association conference). Rumsfeld and Cheney were open in their disdain for lawyers. We went from over-lawyered to lawyer-less.

Executive Order 12333, the one barring the United States from assassinating foreign leaders, had near-canonical status in the intelligence community, and from my point of view, it was an important legal standard worth preserving. It was one of those things that separated Americans from our enemies. But, like other pre-9/11 government strictures, it needed to be reinterpreted for a different set of facts and threats. Targeting a known—or strongly suspected—terrorist operative involved in planning attacks was not the same as assassinating a foreign leader. As with extrajudicial confinement of detainees, the legitimacy of this practice—in which the United States was prosecutor, judge, jury, and executioner—depended on making sure we had the right individual.

The Bush-Cheney policy on targeted killing was based

on the 2001 AUMF, which provided the authority to "kill or capture" terrorists in (or in league with) Al Qaeda. But though the predicate was different, in practice what Bush did was not so different from what his successor did. Obama was always more pragmatic than his most ardent progressive supporters expected—or wanted. During the Bush administration the practice of targeted killings using drones was restrained less by legal concerns than by the limits of the technology and intelligence. Over the years both improved considerably. By the time Obama became president and turned the focus to Al Qaeda in Pakistan, both the CIA and, to a lesser extent, the U.S. military's Joint Special Operations Command (JSOC, an elite cadre of commandos from all the U.S. military services) had become exceptionally agile, accurate, and lethal instruments of national power.

Drones, in particular, are tempting to any commander because of the absence of danger to American pilots or troops on the ground. This was also a key reason cruise missiles became the Clinton administration's weapon of choice. Host countries or human rights groups increasingly protested such missile strikes as the 2000s wore on, but the political blowback was generally minimal. (It was reported that the Pakistani government, despite its harsh public denunciations, secretly supported the strikes and was kept informed with top-secret reports unavailable even to the Congress.)

One of the most controversial tests of this proposition involving an American citizen came in the second year of the Obama administration. By that point my Homeland Security subcommittee was focusing on self-radicalized individuals.

I was increasingly worried that the administration was still neglecting domestic security as Iraq and Afghanistan consumed an ever-growing share of resources and presidential attention. In the case of Anwar al-Awlaki, the "home game" and "away game" converged. Raised in the United States but living in Yemen, Awlaki was reportedly guiding Umar Farouk Abdulmutallab, the Nigerian "underwear bomber" who tried to blow up a jetliner in December 2009. He also had been in contact with Major Nidal Hasan before the U.S. Army major killed thirteen people and wounded more than thirty others at Fort Hood in November 2009. Within the space of a few months Awlaki had gone from near obscurity to "terrorist number one."

By early 2010 Awlaki had been linked to the deaths of dozens of Americans, and could have killed hundreds more. He was recruiting and inspiring others to follow his path, including many aggrieved Muslims in the United States. So the Obama administration approved Awlaki for targeted killing. I agreed that Awlaki could be a target but thought the administration needed to be more open about its rationale and process. Back then we didn't know about the "kill list" of names that would be approved by Obama personally on a case-by-case basis. Consistent with its predecessors, the White House tried to keep the 2010 OLC legal opinion on Awlaki classified and fought off lawsuits by the ACLU and *New York Times* seeking disclosure.

Awlaki was killed in a drone strike on September 30, 2011. By then I had left Congress but was still following the case closely. I told CNN that the "targeted killing of anyone should give us pause," but Awlaki was a "good case" of someone posing an imminent threat. Nonetheless, "the debate on the legal grounds for that strategy should be more in the open."

In place of releasing the internal documents, the White House issued a public white paper—much as the Bush 43 administration had done in responding to the NSA surveillance story. The Obama administration's white paper explained the grounds for killing a U.S. citizen abroad, away from a known war zone like Afghanistan: that the person was an imminent threat to the United States, that there was a danger of this person escaping, and that it was not possible to capture that person alive.

Consistent with its promise to focus on Al Qaeda and minimize troop commitments (after the Afghan military surge), the Obama administration conducted more drone strikes in Pakistan during its first two years than the total number under Bush 43. The criteria for targeted killings expanded over time, from intelligence showing that a particular individual was affiliated with Al Qaeda and involved in attacks to what analysts later called "patterns of life." If reconnaissance showed men of military age behaving over time in a way that was consistent with prior Al Qaeda–linked activity, a "signature strike" was deemed justified. As the aperture of justification widened, the number of strikes predictably rose, as did civilian casualties. Criticism of the practice would grow internationally and among progressive Democrats already disenchanted with Obama's military escalation in Afghanistan. From my perch leading the Wilson Center,

I was growing increasingly concerned as well. Based on my congressional experience and sources in the IC, I knew that the CIA program had been far more judicious and careful than many believe. Still, I worried that the cumulative effect was to further inflame Muslim opinion worldwide against the United States. The images of destroyed houses and mangled bodies were giving Al Qaeda and affiliates plenty of "B-roll" for their recruiting videos. Faisal Shahzad, the Pakistani American arrested for attempting to bomb New York's Times Square in May 2010, reportedly told interrogators that the drone strikes in his home country were in part what had motivated him to join the extremist cause.

At one point the administration considered moving all of the targeted strikes from the CIA to the military's Joint Special Operations Command. The JSOC operated under the legislative authority of Title 10 of the United States Code. The distinction between Title 10 and Title 50 (governing intelligence operations) has direct implications for jurisdiction by Congress. Not every military operation is briefed to the armed services committees (in fact, few are). Covert intelligence operations, on the other hand, must be briefed to the intelligence committees and congressional leadership. Over time the administration perfected the practice of so-called sheep dipping, where military forces do the operation under CIA control. The raid that killed Osama Bin Laden was conducted by Navy SEALs, but the chain of command ran through the CIA director. JSOC falls into the gray zone between traditional military operations and the plausible deniability provided by the CIA. At one point the administration considered turning over the CIA's drone mission to the military, but after some mishaps involving JSOC targeting, that idea was set aside.

Recognizing the criticism, Obama would roll out new presidential policy guidance in May 2013 that acknowledged and formalized the lethal targeting program. Obama was saying the right things, and I wrote that his "course corrections on his drone policy are important." Still, while Obama had spoken about possible "drone courts," the use of drones remained extrajudicial, at the discretion of the president or, in the case of JSOC, the military chain of command. "The executive branch is policing itself—a scary proposition," I commented.

Under more stringent policy application, the number of drone killings began to decrease toward the end of Obama's second term. As part of the administration's stated commitment to more transparency, the DNI later issued a report on estimated civilian casualties from U.S. counterterrorism strikes "outside areas of active hostilities" (i.e., not counting Afghanistan, Iraq, or Syria) between 2009 and 2015. It reported more than 470 strikes killing between 2,300 and 2,600 combatants, and also causing between 64 and 116 "non-combatant deaths." The DNI civilian casualty numbers strained credulity; while assessing civilian collateral damage remotely was difficult, estimates from NGOs were much higher. The rest of the world, including U.S. allies, wasn't buying what we were selling.

In the same 2013 speech focused on the drone program, Obama addressed the broader campaign against terrorism he had inherited: "Unless we discipline our thinking, our defi-nitions, our actions, we may be drawn into more wars we don't need to fight, or continue to grant presidents unbound powers more suited for traditional armed conflicts between nation states." He called for refining "and ultimately repeal-ing" the 2001 AUMF "to determine how we can continue to fight terrorism without keeping America on a perpet-ual wartime footing." With Bin Laden dead, the core of Al Qaeda decimated, and troops being drawn down to below pre-surge levels in Afghanistan, the administration was hop-ing to "pivot" from terrorism and the Middle East to a focus on China and Asia. But events had a way of interfering. The modus operandi of conducting war via presidential action would continue up to the last days of the administration.

A week after I announced my departure from Congress a revolt began in mid-February 2011 against Muammar Gad-dafi in Libya. I was one of the few Americans to have met Gaddafi; it had been during a congressional delegation in 2004. Our small group was based in Tripoli, then the very cosmopolitan capital of Libya, waiting for the call to travel to Sirte, Gaddafi's hometown. The meeting kept being de-layed, and finally I announced we were planning to return home. Shortly thereafter, limos magically appeared to race us through the desert. Gaddafi appeared in Arab garb with what was likely a curly wig under a pillbox hat. His complex-ion was yellow (perhaps jaundice, I thought). Under a huge circus-like tent we were seated on couches; Gaddafi, nursing a bad back, sat on a cheap rigid plastic chair. He was a ruthless dictator with plenty of blood on his hands. But he had also given up Libya's nuclear weapons program after the U.S. intercepted a major shipment from Pakistan and provided intelligence assistance against Al Qaeda. Several years later, Libya became part of the "Arab Spring" narrative—the cause of democracy overcoming tyranny. After Gaddafi cracked down on the rebels, a coalition of Western governments first instituted a no-fly zone over Libya and then undertook air strikes against Gaddafi's forces.

As a presidential candidate, Obama said: "The president does not have power under the Constitution to unilaterally authorize a military attack in a situation that does not involve stopping an actual or imminent threat to the nation." In 2011, Libya did not threaten the United States in any way—quite the contrary, in fact, because the regime had been cooperative. As there was no connection to Al Qaeda, using the 2001 AUMF was implausible. The White House did not invoke the 1973 War Powers Act—the post-Vietnam reform, often violated, which set a sixty-day limit on initiating military hostilities without congressional approval.

In this case it was predominantly our European allies—led by the French—clamoring for military action. The United States was, in the words of an unnamed official, "leading from behind," providing mostly logistical, intelligence, surveillance, and reconnaissance support. Before long, however, the United States was providing a large share of air strikes as well—despite claims that we weren't engaged truly in "hostilities" (which would trigger the War Powers Act). Soon after, the rebels discovered Gaddafi hiding, and executed him; his bullet-ridded body was shown on video being dragged through a ditch. No tears would be shed for Gaddafi.

To the extent Obama sought (or received) any authorization to act in Libya, it was from the UN and NATO, not the U.S. Congress. But our side had won, or seemed to, at minimal American cost in lives or treasure. So Congress was, again, willing to look the other way—at least until the American ambassador to Libya and several other officials were killed in a militant assault in Benghazi a year later.

During this same period Syria was engulfed in a civil war pitting the Assad regime against various militant and rebel groups. One of those groups, ISIS, was so brutal that it was even disowned by Al Qaeda. The president sent out feelers to the Congress regarding an AUMF to stop the wanton bloodshed but found little support from either caucus. Obama then declared his own "red line": Syrian use of chemical weapons. But later the Assad regime crossed this line, without military consequence.

By the end of the summer of 2014 ISIS had conquered large swaths of western and central Iraq, threatening Baghdad at one point. ISIS was achieving what neither Al Qaeda nor the Taliban had been able to accomplish: carving out an Islamic caliphate in the heart of the Middle East. This time Obama did invoke the War Powers Act—first for the purpose of protecting the remaining American personnel in Iraq, then to prevent potential massacres of religious minorities. Obama sent six different war powers resolution letters to the Congress over the summer, each covering a discrete military operation in Iraq. Clinton had done this four times during operations over Bosnia in 1995 as part of a limited series of NATO air strikes to get the Serbs to the negotiating table. Typically, the president would be expected to make one notification to cover an entire military campaign, which would ultimately require congressional authorization to continue. I wrote: "By this otherworldly interpretation, we aren't fighting a war with [ISIS], we're picking a dozen sequential fights with [ISIS] and will continue doing so until the President decides he has achieved his objectives. With all this going on, it's no wonder that we've struggled to craft a coherent response to this depraved band of thugs."

In September 2014 Obama spoke to the country and effectively declared war on ISIS "through a comprehensive and sustained counterterrorism strategy." He "welcomed" congressional support but did not insist on it. In an ironic twist, President Obama proposed an authorization that would actually curb his power by including strict time limits. Republicans were skeptical of giving the president *less* power than what he had already; clearly we had to confront ISIS, and it was going to take a long time. But under what authority could this be done? The White House eventually claimed the authority already existed in the 2001 AUMF because ISIS was the "true heir" to Bin Laden's legacy and was supported by "some individual members and factions of [Al Qaeda]–aligned groups." Following the lead of his predecessor, Obama had made increasing use of his authority as commander in chief under Article II plus the "quaint and seemingly ancient" (as I described it) 2001 AUMF. If Bush and Cheney had done such a thing, my former Democratic colleagues would have been outraged, and justifiably so.

Through a skillful military campaign ISIS was rolled back and eventually smashed. But the precedent was disturbing. The unilateral approach to using military force established by Bush was effectively embellished by Obama—just in time for Trump to become commander in chief.

There are real-world strategic consequences for a White House untethered from the Congress on foreign and security policy. The brutal overthrow of Gaddafi in Libya—after the U.S. and its European allies lobbied for a UN Security Council resolution explicitly without "regime change" as an objective—taught Iran and North Korea that they should keep nuclear weapons if they wanted to survive, because those states without nuclear weapons—Gaddafi had surrendered his—might not. In Syria, there was never much of a chance for regime change or, frankly, any agreeable outcome. But America's failure to act decisively—on the "red line" in particular—provided an opportunity for Russia to become a power player again in the Middle East for the first time in decades.

Additionally, the Trump White House's desire to court and placate Mohammed Bin Salman, the crown prince of Saudi Arabia, by bypassing the Congress to sell U.S. weapons to Saudi Arabia for its intervention in Yemen means that in the eyes of the world, America is now complicit with the humanitarian catastrophe in Yemen. The Trump administration abruptly pulled out of the Iran nuclear accord of its own volition, sending a message to the world—including North Korea and Iran—that America does not honor agreements.

Within the United States, the "muscle memory" of collaboration—between the executive and the legislative, between Republicans and Democrats—has largely faded. Trump nominees for senior federal positions were either confirmed narrowly by party-line votes or rejected. A record number of senior jobs in the federal government—including many in the Pentagon and State Department—were held by acting appointees not fully accountable to the Congress. The dysfunctional relationship between the Trump administration and Congress removed the few remaining guardrails for the White House in national security. We may forget that the problem is not of recent origin; this trend began in the 1990s under President Clinton with U.S. military operations in the Balkans that were pursued without congressional authorization.

There are calls to end the now common practice of making recess appointments to fill positions at the head of federal agencies, and to curb the tendency of presidents to use funding appropriated by Congress for specific purposes to achieve other aims (e.g., DoD funds going to pay for a border wall). Like the ODNI, the White House National Security Council was established to coordinate among government security agencies. After 9/11, the NSC peaked at nearly 400 staff, roughly ten times its size under Bush 41. President Trump fired three national security advisors and ignored any process. President Biden now has the opportunity to rebuild the NSC to restore and enhance its original coordinating function. When Senate-confirmed cabinet secretaries are undermined or bypassed by a micromanaging White House, the result is less oversight by Congress and accountability to the American public.

President Biden, a former chair of the Senate Foreign Relations Committee, has a long history of bipartisanship, having worked even with the most conservative Republicans—a record that caused him some trouble during the Democratic primaries. Reaching across to the other end of Pennsylvania Avenue—and across the aisle on Capitol Hill—is instinctive for Biden in ways that it was not for his former boss, Barack Obama.

But as recent history has shown, even the most genial and enlightened presidents are unlikely to cede power or autonomy voluntarily. Ultimately, only Congress can put a stop to presidential overreach. To meet this responsibility, it will need to overcome the toxic residue of partisanship and dysfunction that has enveloped the institution.

SEVEN

The Incredible
Shrinking Congress

It was December 2004 and we were in the midst of negotiating the final details on legislation to reform America's intelligence community—its biggest overhaul since 1947. Since the bill came from different committees in each chamber—Intelligence in the House and Homeland Security in the Senate—the conference committee structure to resolve differences was somewhat ad hoc. The so-called Big Four were the chairs and ranking members of the two committees: Susan Collins and Joe Lieberman in the Senate, Pete Hoekstra and me in the House. It was the lame-duck session, and we met in the evenings in Speaker Hastert's conference room on the House side of the Capitol. I quipped that Susan Collins and I—the two women—were half the group but did 98 percent of the work. After one late-night session ended, Susan and I decided to go to Bistro Bis for a nightcap. Sitting at a small table near the window, we talked about family and work. While we were deep in conversation, a waiter brought a bottle that was a gift from a man sitting at the bar. We hesitated, not knowing who he was. Then the waiter conveyed the man's message: "You look like sisters having a lovely chat and that is worth celebrating." We agreed. Women in the Congress still continue to display more bipartisanship than others as a general rule. Overall, this kind of ongoing friendship and constructive partnership with someone from the other party has become exceedingly rare.

Congress has not passed an AUMF in nearly two decades or stepped up to its constitutional responsibilities in national security. It has become hobbled by a toxic form of partisanship that took root in the late 1980s. Initial post-9/11 cooperation was followed by government shutdowns, the Tea Party, sequestration, and an impeachment. A growing number in both parties declared bipartisanship a dirty word. The basic functions of governing, including the responsibility to declare war and pass annual appropriations, became an afterthought, a distant second to the goal of winning the next election.

I served more than eight terms in the Congress—that's more than 100 dog years, and it certainly felt that way at times. During that period the U.S. initiated overt military hostilities in at least four countries—Bosnia, Kosovo, Afghanistan, and Iraq; other military actions took place in Libya, Syria, and Iraq (again) shortly after I retired. This tally does not count the kill-or-capture missions conducted by the CIA or special operations forces in other countries. Each time Congress's role seemed to diminish: less involvement, less authority, less responsibility.

What hasn't changed in 230 years is the U.S. Constitution,

which delegates to the Congress, and only the Congress, the power to declare war. A formal U.S. declaration of war hasn't happened since 1942, against Hungary and Romania, then fighting alongside Nazi Germany. Since then the number of times that presidents have used military force far exceeds the number of times Congress has voted to authorize it (in 1964 for Vietnam, 1991 for the Gulf War, 2001 after 9/11, and 2002 for the Iraq War). The 2001 AUMF has been invoked by three presidents to justify forty actions in fourteen countries.

The Senate and House office buildings are named for the great leaders of Congress, including Sam Rayburn and Phil Hart. The landmark 1980s reform of the Pentagon is still referred to by the names of the bipartisan duo (Republican senator Barry Goldwater, Democratic congressman Bill Nichols) whose vision and determination made the legislation possible. The same goes for the successful 1990s effort to secure and dismantle the nuclear weapons of the Soviet Union, led by Democratic senator Sam Nunn and Republican senator Richard Lugar. It is hard to see a current leader in the Congress who stands out in a similar way on national security. In setting up the original balance of powers in the Constitution, the Framers probably did not expect that the legislative branch would become so complicit in its own relative impotence. One culprit is pure self-interest. Providing congressional approval (or rejection) of a war meant casting a vote—one that could be held for or against an incumbent in the next election. Fewer and fewer members want to go on the record voting against a military intervention that may go well (Iraq I) or voting for a war that may go badly (Iraq II). Over the past decade, as America muddled through one hasty intervention after another, most members were content to let the president take the lead and, if something went wrong (as is inevitable in war), take the heat.

I look at what went wrong through the lens of my own experience: how political moderates became first hunted and then an endangered species, caught in the crossfire between the far left and the far right. The punishment for bipartisanship became harsh and immediate. The business model shifted from working together to solve urgent problems facing the country to blaming the other side for not solving the urgent problems. To me this is, sadly, a lose-lose paradigm. This is not just a matter of good governance; it is critical to national security. Nearly every major unmet challenge requires legislation that a majority of both parties can support and that a fair-minded president of either party would sign.

Politics in this country has always been a rough business. The country's first elected officials said and did horrible things to each other on a regular basis: spreading salacious rumors that were printed in partisan pamphlets, or even challenging each other to armed duels. Under Thomas Jefferson a "second revolution" was threatened over the repayment of the national war debt. In the nineteenth century, Massachusetts senator Charles Sumner was nearly caned to death by his South Carolina colleague after giving an abolitionist speech.

Anti-lynching and civil rights legislation went nowhere for decades because of filibusters led by segregationist senators.

There was no halcyon era of civility and bipartisanship. But it is a cop-out to accept what the Congress has become. When I was chief counsel to several Senate Judiciary Committee subcommittees in the mid-1970s, bills were negotiated and passed, usually with bipartisan majorities. Politicians went at it during campaigns and would castigate each other in the press—then quietly go back to work holding hearings on complex subjects and negotiating finer points of legislation. Budgets were for the most part passed on time, albeit with eleventh-hour negotiating. Differences were hammered out with legislative horse-trading—a sometimes grubby but necessary part of governing. Agreements across the aisle would be reached and then enforced by the veteran leaders in each party. Leaders like Ted Kennedy, Bob Dole, Phil Hart, Howard Baker, Tom Foley, and Bob Michel (in those days, the leaders were all men) knew when to put politics aside, at least temporarily, to get something done. There continue to be good people in both parties who are frustrated by the broken business model both parties now employ. But the dysfunction continues because blaming the other side for not solving the problem seems to be the best ticket to reelection.

I remember well a different world. At age fifteen I stood on the Democratic National Convention floor in 1960 when John F. Kennedy was nominated for president. Kennedy's call to a new generation of leadership to ask what they could do for their country is inspirational still. The politicking part of politics held little appeal for me, both then and now. The draw was how government policy could change lives and protect our country. Politics was the mechanism for getting in a position to make good policy happen.

It is hard to describe to a young person what the late 1960s were like—the body count from Vietnam and the rifts it created even among families, riots that gutted several major cities, the assassinations of John and Robert Kennedy and Martin Luther King Jr. It's also true that when Watergate happened, the congressional inquiry was bipartisan and the impeachment vote by the House Judiciary Committee was bipartisan. That was the Congress I joined as a staffer for California senator John Tunney in 1972. It was also largely the Congress I joined as an elected representative in 1993.

In retrospect, I see that the slide toward zero-sum, ad hominem politics had already begun. Negative campaign ads had been around since the dawn of television, but they were perfected and exploited in the 1980s to maximum effect by GOP operative Lee Atwater (his two lobbying partners then were Roger Stone and Paul Manafort). The shift to building single-party majorities was under way. My Republican friends will respond by citing the campaign to block the confirmation of Robert Bork to the Supreme Court in 1987, and they have a point. One could take issue with Bork's judicial philosophy—I likely would have voted against him if I had been in the Senate—but not his qualifications. Instead he was attacked personally and his legal writings caricatured beyond recognition. A new verb entered the political lexicon: "to Bork." (A Republican nominee with a very similar judicial philosophy, Antonin Scalia, had been confirmed 98–0 the year before.)

The Clarence Thomas–Anita Hill hearings were the backdrop when I was running for Congress in 1992; women were outraged at the smearing of Hill. In the November election, a huge turnout by pro-choice women helped me win and brought about the first "Year of the Woman" in the U.S. Congress—we nearly doubled the number of women in the House, and my home state elected two female senators, Barbara Boxer and Dianne Feinstein. My district, which included Palos Verdes and Torrance, leaned Republican; Maureen Reagan, the moderate, pro-choice daughter of the former president, lost the Republican primary, but had she won, she almost certainly would have defeated me in the general election. Her brain trust became known as "Republicans for Harman." Back then overt support from members of the other party was not a political liability.

I was a "New Democrat": pro-defense and (especially important for my district) pro-aerospace, but also an unapologetic social progressive, strongly pro-choice and pro-LGBTQ rights, back when the latter was a riskier proposition than it is today. I voted against the homophobic Defense of Marriage Act in 1996 and recall that Nancy Pelosi, even back then protective of Democratic incumbents as she aimed to build a potential majority, said she feared my vote might cost me in the next election. Counterintuitively for a moderate, pro-business Democrat, I voted against the North American Free Trade Agreement. My concern was that the lack of labor

and environmental requirements in the agreement would put
American companies and workers at an unfair disadvantage
(which would cause the "giant sucking sound" of jobs dis-
appearing from the United States, as Ross Perot put it). I
worked with Californians of all political stripes, including
Republican governor Pete Wilson, to mitigate the impact of
deep defense and intelligence spending cuts on the aerospace
industry in our state, through promoting dual-use commercial applications and, with an eye on the future, fighting to
sustain investment in modernization R&D.

By the time I arrived in the Congress, the style of cam-
paigning had already changed—but Congress still legislated.
Then came the earthquake of 1994. The Democrats' majority
was gone; most of the women elected to open seats in 1992,
as I had been, lost. I squeaked to reelection by 811 votes out
of more than 200,000 cast. Newt Gingrich and his "Contract
with America" reflected a new, winner-take-all mentality.
That's when Congress began to change in ways large and small.

The first major test of this all-or-nothing approach
ended in the long government shutdown of 1995, a strategic
blunder for the Republicans. President Clinton adroitly piv-
oted to the center with welfare reform, handily won reelection, and built a bipartisan majority to balance the budget in
1997. Whatever rapport existed between the parties in the
Congress and between the Congress and the White House
was blown up again with the Monica Lewinsky scandal
and the resulting impeachment proceedings. Impeachment
sucked all the oxygen out of everything else—including, om-
inously, the U.S. effort against Al Qaeda—and government

ground to a halt. It was in this context that I decided to leave the Congress and run for governor in 1998. Senator Dianne Feinstein, the presumptive Democratic front-runner, had decided not to run, and her would-be campaign team (along with my husband, Sidney), strongly encouraged me to pick up the baton.

It was a rugged twelve-week, three-way primary. My campaign ads were all positive, and after six weeks I was first in the polls. Then one opponent unleashed a withering $42 million ad blitz distorting all my congressional votes. It was called a "murder-suicide," and the result was that the third candidate, Gray Davis, came out on top. My open seat in Congress was then won by a moderate Republican who was a former state legislator. The Democrats were hoping to re-take the House in 2000, which would require winning over moderate Republicans in districts such as mine. Having won three times before, I was considered the best shot to put my former seat back in the Democrat column. In the end, Adam Schiff and I were two of only four Democrats who flipped Republican seats, and the Republicans kept the majority. The partisan climate when I returned was worse due in part to the 2000 Florida recount and the 5–4 *Bush v. Gore* Supreme Court decision. All the more galling was that the new Bush administration plowed ahead with a conservative agenda as if they'd just won a landslide.

To persuade me to run again, the Democratic leadership had promised in writing to restore my seniority on HPSCI, which put me in line to chair the committee following Julian Dixon, who tragically died at the end of 2000, and Nancy Pelosi, who was widely expected to be elected to House leadership with my strong support (it is customary that elected leaders do not also hold senior positions on committees).

In spring 2001 I was appointed co-chair of the newly formed Speaker's Working Group on International Terrorism and Homeland Security. My counterpart was Georgia Republican Saxby Chambliss. We were somewhat the odd couple. Elected in the 1994 Gingrich wave that took out many southern Democrats, he was the son of an Episcopalian minister and had a deep southern drawl. I was the socially progressive Ivy Leaguer from Los Angeles by way of New York and D.C. But we formed an effective working partnership—and an enduring friendship.

On the morning of 9/11, it was to Saxby's apartment that we went after the Capitol was evacuated and a group of us were left milling about on the lawn, sitting ducks for any follow-on attack. Later that day, while the congressional top leadership was still stranded in undisclosed locations (built during the Cold War with a Soviet nuclear attack in mind), our working group held a brief press conference at Capitol Police headquarters. I was appalled that on the most traumatic day in American history the United States Congress had effectively shut down and gone silent. So I opened my statement by saying, "As you can see, Congress is open for business." I wanted the public to know that we hadn't simply melted away but had been monitoring the situation and were focused on taking action to prevent further damage. Nine days later our working group was elevated to full subcommittee status, which meant we could hold hearings and call witnesses. After that announcement I said, "There's no way Congress can continue any sort of partisan bickering on this issue, and we won't."

Saxby and I recognized that party politics and affiliations would intrude from time to time. Later we would disagree on the administration's surveillance and interrogations policy. But our differences never got in the way of finding common ground to protect our country, especially in those early months. "I could not have asked for a ranking member to work in a more cooperative manner than Jane has with me," he told the *Los Angeles Times* in January 2002. "There are obviously things you have to do from a partisan standpoint from time to time. But HPSCI has always worked on a bipartisan basis and that has carried over to this subcommittee." A bill we co-sponsored on information sharing passed the House 422–2.

Nonetheless, during the 2002 midterms an outside group funded a vicious campaign ad against incumbent Democratic senator Max Cleland of Georgia, who was being challenged by Chambliss for that Senate seat. Cleland had lost three limbs in Vietnam but was attacked in the ad as weak on terrorism for supporting civil service protections for the workforce of the new Department of Homeland Security. Cleland, my friend from the days when he was Veterans Affairs administrator and I worked in the Carter White House, lost. For me, Saxby's victory was bittersweet. The White House had pushed for the Iraq War vote to take place just before the midterms, with Bush still near the peak of his popularity and the country still fearful of another attack. These were cynical maneuvers marring a period of otherwise constructive bipartisan activity culminating in the establishment of DHS in December 2002.

HPSCI continued to work in a bipartisan manner for a while longer. As late as 2003, Porter Goss and I were co-signing letters to the White House demanding a better explanation on Iraqi WMD. In the summer of 2004 Pete Hoekstra, also an advocate for reforming the intelligence community, would become HPSCI chair. As described earlier, our dogged bipartisan effort would overcome entrenched opposition by the Pentagon and GOP conservatives to produce the most important intelligence legislation in nearly a half century. One factor in our success: Senators Collins and Lieberman agreed from the start that any differences we had over the bill would be handled in private. We would present a united bipartisan front to the Government Affairs and Homeland Security Committee, the respective caucuses, the White House, and the news media. After the final vote approving the intelligence reform legislation in December 2004, the Speaker of the House gave Hoekstra and me each a wood gavel recognizing our roles in getting the legislation passed—a classy gesture that reflected one of the remaining strengths of Congress at the time.

The House and Senate intelligence committees continued to be what I called "islands of bipartisan sanity"—especially compared to ideological battlegrounds like Judiciary. I often said, and still do, that the terrorists won't check our party registration before they blow us up. There was plenty of argument, sometimes heated, over the NSA surveillance program or the appropriate way to handle interrogations. But it was driven by differences over policy and ideology, not by partisan or personal animosity.

The Senate was far less partisan than the House. Legislators of the "old school" GOP, like John Warner, Richard Lugar, and Pat Roberts, would strive for bipartisanship given the important national security responsibilities of their committees. In February 2006, Pat Roberts and I appeared together on *Meet the Press*, and he said, "I don't mean to pick a fuss with my good friend Jane, who I agree with 90 percent of the time." The opening of a May 26 hearing provided another example of collegiality after Hoekstra stumbled on a multisyllabic word in his opening statement:

HARMAN: It's a big word for a Republican.
  [*Laughter.*]
HOEKSTRA: Thank you, Ms. Harman. [*Laughter.*]
  You know, we like to help each other. Jane is here
  to help.

The dialogue continued after we each gave opening statements:

HARMAN: Thank you, Mr. Chairman. . . .
    I am pleased to hear you quoting from
    my remarks in your opening statement.
HOEKSTRA: We hang on every word.
HARMAN: I think that's a very good start.
    You might, next time, just give my opening
    statement [*laughter*] . . . and then we'll,
    I think, both be enlightened. [*Laughter.*]

Finding areas of agreement and paying compliments were a regular feature of my exchanges with Hoekstra and other Republicans in hearings or in television appearances. Hoekstra had shown impressive independence since taking over the committee from Porter Goss. He openly opposed the nomination of General Mike Hayden, George W. Bush's pick as CIA director, because of his status as an active-duty military officer. (The House does not confirm presidential nominees, so Hoekstra was not forced to formally vote against a president from his own party.) Then, in May, Hoekstra wrote a letter to Bush objecting in unusually strong terms to the administration's pattern of withholding briefings on the most highly classified code-word programs. Hoekstra and I would hear about the programs for the first time from our IC contacts, which was not how the process was supposed to work. (In another increasingly rare sign of independence, the Senate leadership had forced the White House to start briefing the full intelligence committees—something I had long been pressing for—as a condition of getting Hayden confirmed.)

With the Hurricane Katrina disaster still fresh and the situation in Iraq getting worse, the White House and Republican leadership became increasingly worried about the November 2006 midterm election. Efforts to put a positive spin on the war went to farcical extremes. Hoekstra allowed himself to get roped into a press conference in which Senator Rick Santorum, a Pennsylvania Republican, declared that Saddam had WMD after all. A few rounds of mustard gas and chemical munitions had been found; they dated back to the 1980s, left over from the Iran-Iraq War. Nothing close to the claims used to justify the U.S. invasion.

The White House reverted to tried-and-true political winners: hyping potential terror threats and invoking 9/11 at every opportunity. In a report marking the fifth anniversary of the attacks, the administration extolled its "victories" in the war on terror, though it played down the importance of Osama Bin Laden (who was still at large) and the role of the invasion of Iraq in exacerbating the threat. A week later, the HPSCI majority staff dutifully released its own unclassified report based on public sources (mostly news media) that were largely supportive of the administration's positions. I authorized the release of a separate Democratic minority report that characterized the majority product as "merely an assemblage of press clippings" offering nothing new: "[The report] cherry-picks and gives a picture that is less than complete . . . the timing here fits the election calendar."

Hoekstra opened the press conference for the majority

report by invoking the story of Rick Rescorla, a decorated Vietnam combat veteran; a photo of Rescorla holding a fixed bayonet was one of the most iconic images of that war. Rescorla was head of security for Morgan Stanley when he died on 9/11, having warned repeatedly over the previous several years of a possible terrorist attack on the World Trade Center towers. His was one of the most evocative and heartbreaking stories from that terrible day. The majority's message was blinking red: better vote Republican to stop that from happening again. The shamelessness of the GOP on terrorism was disappointing given my respect for Pete and many of his colleagues. It was also strange. The worst terror attack in U.S. history happened on the Bush administration's watch, and their major post-9/11 initiative (the invasion of Iraq) made the terror threat worse. Yet the polls showed that terrorism was viewed as a Republican advantage. The widespread expectation of planned follow-on Al Qaeda attacks worked to the administration's advantage, as it allowed the White House to take credit for the absence of another major attack since.

Still, as late as September, Hoekstra told NPR: "Jane and I have really tried to maintain a very, very good relationship. You know, we like each other personally. When it looks like it's taking a turn to go ugly, we'll sit down and we'll try to get it back on course." Mike Hayden invited us to dinner at his stately general officer's house in Fort McNair. The dinner occurred after one of our rare fights. Pete and I glared at each other across the table.

Then, toward the end of the month, the *New York Times*

ran a story based on sources who had prepared or reviewed the NIE on global terrorism. The assessment concluded that the Iraq War had become a rallying cry for Islamic extremists, "breeding a deep resentment of US involvement in the Muslim world and cultivating supporters for the global jihadist movement." The White House tried to provide "context" for the story two days later by declassifying and releasing more of its principal findings. The administration was still clinging to the line that fighting the terrorists in Iraq ("there") was necessary to avoid them in the United States ("here"). In a statement I said, "The opposite is true. Because we are fighting them there, it may become more likely that we'll have to fight them here." I added, "[The NIE] paints a grim picture. And because it does, I am told it is being held until after the November elections. If this estimate is finished, it should not be stamped 'draft' and hidden from the American people."

It was in that fevered environment that I took a step that, in the words of a *Washington Post* editorial, was sure to be "thermonuclear." Without Hoekstra's assent I released an executive summary of a committee report about former representative (and HPSCI member) Randy "Duke" Cunningham. The sad story of Cunningham—a former naval fighter ace during the Vietnam War who was convicted of taking more than $2 million in bribes as a congressman—has been well told elsewhere. Hoekstra and I had agreed that an investigation was merited into what, if any, help Cunningham received from committee staff in his wrongdoing. Before the investigation we also agreed to make the findings public. Then Hoekstra and the GOP staff began to change their minds. The Democratic members of HPSCI urged me to honor the agreement to release a summary. I redacted all staff names, and did it.

The conviction of Cunningham—who had begun recently serving an eight-year sentence—was yet another black eye for the Republican majority after the revelations that Florida representative Mark Foley had sent explicit messages to teenage congressional pages. The Jack Abramoff lobbying scandals would send another Republican member to prison and implicate two aides of Tom DeLay, the House majority leader. Ending the "culture of corruption" was a major Democratic theme for the midterms. Still, it was a tough call to release the redacted summary of the Cunningham report given my long-standing commitment to bipartisan cooperation on that committee.

Hoekstra hit the roof. What I did not expect, even in the political acrimony of the time, was what came next—that same day, in fact. Hoekstra suspended the access to classified materials of the Democratic staffer accused of leaking the global terrorism NIE in advance of the *New York Times* article. Then it was my turn to be furious. If Hoekstra wanted to get back at me, so be it. But taking it out on a staffer was unconscionable. I told NPR, "This is real personal. And my point is that if members want to fight among each other, at least we signed up for this. But to retaliate against innocent staff is just reckless and irresponsible." The *Washington Post* editorialized: "Ms. Harman's unilateral strike violated the bipartisan basis on which the intelligence committees are meant, at least in theory, to operate. But that cannot justify

Mr. Hoekstra's malicious and misdirected response, which tarnished a staff member's reputation and was not supported by any evidence." Hoekstra went on to propose an extensive internal inquiry—a fishing expedition, really—looking at staff emails and phone records to find any unauthorized contacts with the media. After the election he would reinstate the staffer, who by now was represented by Jonathan Turley, a George Washington University law professor who would rise to prominence later for his opposition to the Trump impeachment. In the interim, the staffer worked in my personal office handling nonclassified duties.

During this period HPSCI was also at an impasse over FISA legislation. At the end of the summer I said, "Our committee on a party line vote reported out a bill that allows for broad eavesdropping on Americans in violation of the Fourth Amendment. . . . The committee has become a partisan tool designed to improve Republican chances in the November elections."

The media firestorm years later about NSA wiretapping and my relationship with AIPAC had its origins in this period of growing partisanship and animosity on the committee. That story first appeared toward the end of October 2006. This was on the heels of a very nasty public dispute with the HPSCI majority over the Cunningham report, and just a couple of weeks before the congressional midterms.

The same basic story was dredged up nearly four years later and given new life with the allegations of NSA wiretaps (described in Chapter 5). On the day the *New York Times* ran the inflammatory front-page article, Senator Susan Collins (by then my close friend) was coming to my house near Rock Creek Park for dinner. I was afraid the press would be camped out in my driveway and would catch Susan coming and going, which could make things awkward for her. I told her we should probably reschedule the long-planned dinner for some other time. Susan would have none of it and came over as planned.

Harry Truman famously said that if you want a friend in Washington, get a dog. In my experience, if you want a friend in Washington, get a girlfriend. Some of my closest friendships have been with women colleagues, and with one mentor who served before me and played an outsize role in my approach to politics and life. I met Geraldine Ferraro in 1984 when she selected me to be outside counsel to the Democratic platform committee, which she chaired. She was one of Speaker Tip O'Neill's favorites, and the exposure she received in that role catapulted her to be the first female vice presidential nominee on a major-party ticket. Gerry and I became the greatest of friends, and I was honored to speak alongside both Clintons, Fritz Mondale, and Madeleine Albright at her funeral in 2011. Gerry combined high intelligence with wit and humor, a style I have tried to emulate. And to her core she put the country and her wonderful family first.

Susan Collins became engaged for the first time at age fifty-nine, and I hosted her huge bipartisan engagement party at my D.C. home. She tried on potential wedding dresses at my house, and I was a guest at her small and lovely family wedding in Caribou, Maine, a small town at the farthest reaches of New England. Susan is one of the last bipartisan deal-makers left in the Senate and the sole New England Republican in either chamber. She has survived the political fight of her life and remains a strong voice for bipartisanship.

Other mentors and friends include Dianne Feinstein, whom I met when she was mayor of San Francisco and who remains my buddy in the intel enterprise; Debbie Dingell, who was spouse to the legendary John Dingell, another mentor of mine, and now serves with distinction in his old district; Karen Bass, who chaired the Congressional Black Caucus and has a huge future in the House and elsewhere; Kirsten Gillibrand, who famously went into labor in a HASC mark-up session and is my tennis partner; and Heather Wilson and Zoe Lofgren, whom I mentioned earlier. I also dearly miss Ellen Tauscher, a moderate Democrat representing suburban areas east of San Francisco, who went on to be undersecretary of state and tragically died of cancer in 2019.

Since leaving the Congress I've enjoyed getting to know some of the new rising stars. One in particular is Elissa Slotkin, a former CIA officer (with tours in Iraq) and senior defense policy official who pulled off a remarkable 2018 victory running in a mostly pro-Trump Michigan district. Elissa sticks to principles but also understands the need for—indeed, the virtue of—pragmatism and bipartisan compromise. Unfortunately, those qualities seem to be the exception in the House these days, in both caucuses.

I never hid my strong desire to chair HPSCI. I had spent years learning the sprawling and at times byzantine U.S. intelligence apparatus: its unique terminology, customs, and folkways. I regularly visited CIA stations overseas and had brown-bag lunches with the rank and file. I knew people up and down the org charts of the different IC components, who provided important perspective and information not always forthcoming from the politically appointed leadership. I could spot quickly the holes and deceptions in an NIE or congressional briefing.

The House Democratic leadership, headed by Dick Gephardt, had promised me in writing that I would retain my seniority on HPSCI and become chair when the Democrats took the majority. Six years later, Gephardt was gone and Nancy Pelosi was the Democratic majority leader. By early 2006 I had learned—through word of mouth and news articles—that Pelosi was planning not to elevate me to HPSCI chair. I asked for a meeting in person. We sat across from each other in her spacious office and I expressed my interest in becoming the HPSCI committee chair. She said House rules limited service on HPSCI to eight years, so not only could I not be chair, I would have to leave the committee. I knew that the rules had been changed by House Republicans in 2003 to allow Porter Goss to stay on as HPSCI chair—the term limits no longer applied to the chair or ranking member. Then I mentioned the letter signed by Gephardt and others in 1999. Her response was that *she* hadn't signed the letter. It was her call, and I'd have to live with it.

I was not unsympathetic to the dilemmas Pelosi faced. She was trying to manage a broad center-left majority and its constituent factions. But the pundits and wags could not resist making personal comparisons between two female Democratic representatives from California. Commentary would follow about our biographies, education, wealth, and personal style. What's both curious—and, in many ways, tragic—is that Pelosi and I started out as mutually support-ive allies. We were both at the 1960 Democratic convention but never crossed paths—I was a volunteer usher for John F. Kennedy's acceptance speech at the Los Angeles Coliseum, and she was a part of Democratic Party nobility as a member of the D'Alessandro clan, which dominated Baltimore pol-itics for decades. We met in the 1980s when she became a top fundraiser and head of the California Democratic Party. Having entered the Congress in 1987, Pelosi encouraged me to run in 1992 and was a great source of advice and sup-port throughout. When I left Congress in 1998 to run for governor of California, Pelosi threw me a hot fudge sundae party in the House members' dining room. She was there at the funeral of my father in 1998, and she and her hus-band, Paul, were at my Aspen home in 2003 to celebrate Sidney's eighty-fifth birthday. I hosted a fundraiser in Los Angeles for her campaign for minority whip that brought in $400,000.

Ultimately it came down to differences in policy—and politics. Pelosi, representing liberal San Francisco, was a strong opponent of the Iraq War and pretty much everything the Bush administration did. I represented an equally authentic tradition in the Democratic Party embodied by JFK and Scoop Jackson. A number of newspapers editorialized and ran op-eds by national security experts favoring my appointment as HPSCI chair. Some expressed incredulity at the other names being mentioned as Pelosi favorites for such a consequential committee.

Ultimately Pelosi chose Texan Silvestre Reyes, an amiable former Border Patrol agent—and, importantly, someone who voted against the Iraq War. I had worked well with Reyes in the past. Wanting to see a smooth transition, I prepared a long memo full of recommendations from my eight years on HPSCI. Still, I was sorely disappointed at not being chosen chair (still no woman!), and I believe I would have made a substantial contribution.

Despite that difficult episode I never stopped admiring Nancy for her trailblazing accomplishments and prodigious political skills. Some fourteen years after first taking the Speaker's gavel, Pelosi has established her place as one of the most effective House leaders in U.S. history. Her handling of the Trump administration and her own diverse caucus has been masterful. On a personal note, Nancy and I share a devotion to family and we often chat at the hairdresser about what our grandkids are doing. I am proud to know her.

As has been discussed earlier, I would go on to have four rewarding and productive years as chair of the Homeland Security Committee's Subcommittee on Intelligence, Information Sharing, and Terrorism Risk Assessment, a position that overlapped much of HPSCI's jurisdiction. Then, a mentor and former chair of the House Foreign Affairs Committee, Lee Hamilton, decided to retire as head of the Wilson Center, and I was selected to succeed him (the first woman in that post). The chance to head a respected bipartisan think tank was too great an opportunity to pass up.

It's also true that by 2011 Congress had entered an era of gridlock and dysfunction that would make the Gingrich Revolution look like bipartisan temperance. Obama's original call for a new tone in Washington had enormous resonance at the time—quite a number of Republicans, including those who voted against him, felt proud to see an African American as the president of the United States. He tried for a while and then gave up (too soon, in my view). The 2010 midterms ushered in a Republican House majority with a new class of Tea Party members opposed to compromise. Incumbent Republican members, including those with solid conservative voting records, were taken down in primaries by Tea Party challengers. Richard Lugar, arguably the Senate's leading foreign policy expert, was defeated in the Indiana primary. Bob Bennett of Utah lost in the primary to libertarian Mike Lee. Mike Castle, a moderate Republican congressman and presumptive favorite to replace Joe Biden as Delaware's senator, came up short against a candidate who had to reassure voters that "I am not a witch."

Many Democrats, relieved to keep the Senate after being swamped in the House, were happy to see Republican incumbents taken out by conservatives more likely to lose as general election candidates. Additionally, the *Citizens United* Supreme Court decision only amplified the role of money and attack ads in elections, giving rise to the unaccountable super PAC. Without candidates or parties to take responsibility for ads, politics grew more vitriolic, not just on TV but through microtargeted ads across social media and the internet. During my final months in the Congress, I watched with bafflement as the 2007 lightbulb-efficiency law that I co-authored with a senior Republican became a Tea Party punching bag. (Even my co-author later voted against it.) What had been the routine raising of the national debt ceiling—reflecting the taxes and expenditures already enacted—was used by House Republicans to threaten a government shutdown in the absence of further cuts. We still haven't recovered from the automatic, across-the-board sequestration cuts in 2013 made to every discretionary function of government, from military training and procurement to the Federal Aviation Administration and the Centers for Disease Control.

HPSCI would eventually recover much of its reputation—at least for a few years—under Republican chair Mike Rogers and ranking Democrat Dutch Ruppersberger. But subsequently, the elevation of Republican Devin Nunes, a fierce Trump loyalist—I once referred to him as a "wrecking ball" on TV—to ranking member would turn the committee into ground zero for the Russia collusion investigation. One small but telling episode stands out. In March 2017, Nunes discovered that the Trump campaign had been subject to electronic surveillance during the previous presidential election. Nunes immediately ran to the White House to share the news with Trump's staff, and possibly the president himself. On CNN, I asserted that Pete Hoekstra, also on the program with me that day, would have shared the information with me first, as ranking member. I certainly would have shared it with him if the roles had been reversed. Hoekstra then noted a former colleague had once told him: "Pete, you would have had a huge price to pay if you would have gone somewhere and you hadn't told Jane about it." He continued: "Congress is a different place . . . than how Jane and I worked and how Congress worked in 2004, 2005, and 2006."

The Russia investigation dragged along for the next two years—Republicans refusing to admit Trump did anything wrong, Democrats unwilling to concede that the FBI had overreached. "Oh, I'm just despondent. The process absolutely stinks," I said on MSNBC. "And we're watching the slow, sad death of the House Intelligence Committee."

HPSCI would later become the epicenter for the Trump impeachment inquiry. I supported both the inquiry and impeachment as necessary. But seeing it all play out in a theatrically partisan fashion was painful for someone like me, who genuinely revered the traditions of that committee and its importance to America's national security.

Over the last decade America's repeated federal budget standoffs and political dysfunction have weakened our reputation internationally, emboldened potential adversaries, and made our economy more vulnerable. We're playing a hyperpartisan game with real ammunition.

The coronavirus crisis of 2020 demonstrates that government competence and capacity still matter, as do congressional action and oversight. As mentioned earlier, the terrorists don't check our party registration before they try to kill us, and the same is true with COVID-19.

It is ironic that some of the dysfunction we are struggling with today is related to prior attempts to reform the election process. The McCain-Feingold Act of 2002 outlawed unlimited inflows of "soft money" to political parties, but its effect was to divert funding to independent third-party groups that are less accountable. Congress eliminated earmarks after a series of pork-barrel scandals, but in so doing removed one of the most effective tools of legislative deal-making.

The House has become significantly more decentralized in the years since a few committee chairmen, known as "old bulls," ran the place with an iron fist. But this means that party leaders have less leverage over their own members—a fact that fatally undermined Speaker John Boehner as he tried to negotiate a budget agreement with President Obama to avoid the draconian effects of so-called "sequestration."

Those who take political risk to work on a bipartisan basis to put country over party should be rewarded, not penalized. As a starting point, congressional districts must become more competitive. I always faced tough elections, in the early years especially, and that reinforced my inclination toward bipartisanship. It will take years to undo the damage of gerrymandering, in which the boundaries of congressional districts are drawn in ways to create dominance for one party or the other. Redistricting is handled at the state level, which makes nationwide changes difficult. Yet several states, including California, have shown a willingness to turn the process over to nonpartisan commissions. The key is to elect more bridge-builders and dealmakers who want to solve problems, instead of just blaming the other party.

Just imagine how much value Congress could add to the intelligence and national security enterprise if capable members in both parties work together. Sufficient funding and rigorous oversight of critical government functions could help prevent or mitigate the impacts of future pandemics, terror plots, or cyberattacks. A reformed committee structure could help ensure that homeland security is not treated like an afterthought. On a regular basis, Congress could adjust the legal framework around surveillance to accommodate new technology. It could right-size the defense budget to focus on the highest-priority threats while restoring funding for soft power and rehabilitating a seriously anemic State Department. The intelligence committees in both chambers could reclaim their role as bipartisan overseers of our nation's most sensitive secrets and national security operations. Broad congressional support of a sound legal framework could ensure that vital intelligence is collected from terror suspects, and other nonmilitary combatants are treated in a manner consistent with American values and international obligations. It all adds up to Congress responsibly exercising its significant constitutional powers—and sworn duties—to provide for the common defense. The result would be a saner government, and a safer America.

Afterword

President Biden cautions that the pandemic is far from over. After a bungled early government response the death toll mounted until vaccines began to have an impact. Additionally, we've been through another presidential impeachment (the fourth in my professional lifetime), a brush with another major war in the Middle East, and mass protests (some violent) convulsing our major cities in ways not seen since the 1960s. These events have only reinforced my convictions leading to this book.

The COVID-19 crisis—unlike 9/11, Hurricane Katrina, and the 2008 financial meltdown—was a calamity we long saw coming. The U.S. government had studied, planned for, and was equipped—at least for a while—to deal with a major pandemic. Work began during the Clinton administration, which created the National Pharmaceutical Stockpile (renamed the Strategic National Stockpile in 2003). In 2006 the Congress created the Biomedical Advanced Research and Development Authority (BARDA) to purchase and develop drugs, vaccines, and diagnostic tools. A bipartisan independent commission provided repeated warnings and recommendations on the impact of a viral outbreak[4]—whether natural or man-made. (It was akin to having the Kean-Hamilton Commission report come out *before* 9/11.) The SARS, MERS, Ebola, and H1N1 swine flu outbreaks provided a preview of what would come later at a more global and lethal scale. The new Obama administration handled H1N1 competently—certainly compared to the Trump administration's COVID-19 response—but there were plenty of shortcomings and lessons learned. These were incorporated into extensive plans developed by the Obama National Security Council.

Focusing the blame for the COVID-19 fiasco exclusively on the Trump administration does not get to the deeper structural problems, many of which are discussed in this book. Article I of the Constitution provides the power of the purse exclusively to the Congress. Yet multiple Congresses, despite ample warnings from outside experts and administration officials, failed to allocate funds sufficient to replenish the National Strategic Stockpile that had been drawn down during H1N1. The Trump White House ignored or discarded the pandemic plans they inherited—along with most other transition recommendations and priorities from the Obama team. There is a tendency of incoming administrations to disregard or seek to do the opposite of their predecessors. The incoming Bush 43 team mostly disregarded

---

4 Bob Graham and Jim Talent, Commission on the Prevention of Weapons of Mass Destruction Proliferation and Terrorism, December 2008. Follow-up "report card" in "U.S. Gets 'F' in Bioterror Response," CNN, January 26, 2010, https://www.cnn .com/2010/POLITICS/01/26/security.report.card/index.html.

warnings about Al Qaeda (the Obama White House was not completely immune from this tendency either). Then there is the bureaucracy—bound by its own rules and culture—that may be full of experience and expertise, but needs a push to change or respond to new circumstances. The Centers for Disease Control was set up, funded, and staffed with thousands of brilliant minds for the principal purpose of handling a major pandemic. Without a sense of urgency and direction from above, the CDC muddled through the first weeks of the outbreak trying to get a working COVID-19 test.

Meanwhile, since the first draft of this book was completed, FISA extension legislation that permits lawful surveillance to protect America remains stalled; ISIS leaders have begun indoctrinating a new generation of jihadists in Kurdish-run prison camps; the Department of Homeland Security is on life support; and negotiations with the Taliban to end the U.S. military presence in Afghanistan are bogged down in a new wave of violence.

Democratic societies focused on day-to-day concerns (and appetites) tend not to confront serious underlying problems until disaster strikes. And since 9/11, our attention span—exacerbated by cable news and social media—has kept shrinking. From my perspective, the shortcomings described in this book stem ultimately from a failure of *political will*—the determination to do the right thing even when there is no great political benefit and when there is potentially a real political cost. It would require Republican adults standing up to the Freedom Caucus to make sure essential health and safety functions of government get properly funded. It would require incoming White House officials to transition out of campaign mode and be willing to admit that their predecessors did some things right (like prioritizing counterterrorism and pandemic planning). Senior government leaders, political appointees or career employees, would have to be willing to say "no," and if necessary, leave, when told by the White House to execute policies or appoint unqualified people who will put the country at greater risk. And, members of Congress would need to put country over party.

In recent years, in the absence of a functioning executive-legislative relationship, the federal courts have played a bigger role. The Supreme Court has issued a series of decisions that demonstrate an ability to compromise and address complex issues in a pragmatic way. This included curbing—but not voiding—the Trump administration's early immigration restrictions; fending off another attempt to overturn *Roe v. Wade*; achieving a middle ground on a controversial Clean Water Act issue; then, giving neither the White House nor congressional Democrats what they wanted with respect to President Trump's tax returns. Chief Justice John Roberts, in particular, seems to have become a genuine institutionalist. For that he's become the target of increasingly hostile attacks from the right and, for a time, from President Trump himself.

This book is full of suggestions for better processes and better policy—both of which are crucial. The issues are hard and the solutions are complicated. Political will to defend the tough options is essential. But the executive branch won't heal itself. Nor, sadly, will Congress. And we cannot expect the courts to keep saving the other two branches from themselves. Hopefully the Biden administration and Democratically controlled Congress will make headway.

The great disruption created by the pandemic has provided new energy and opportunities. The Black Lives Matter movement is an interesting study. It has mobilized a multi-racial sustained protest against systemic racism. But the movement isn't political: those involved are not endorsing candidates and haven't even picked one leader. While clearly on the political left, BLM is not firmly connected with the Democratic Party to push a legislative agenda forward (as did the civil rights leaders with Kennedy and Johnson during the 1960s). Perhaps this demonstrates deep disillusionment with both political parties and an interest in inventing something new. However, it was the ultimate establishment candidate, Joe Biden, who won the Democratic Party nomination and then the presidency in 2020.

The last great expansion of broadly shared prosperity, social progress, and global leadership for the United States was propelled in the aftermath of World War II. If nothing else, the scale of human misery caused by COVID-19—unemployment, isolation, bankruptcy, and more—is forcing a profound change in priorities. The kind of discretionary U.S. military adventurism described in this book is now almost unthinkable. The behavior of China—including its deception on COVID-19—is forcing the United States and European and Asian democracies to bond in ways that we haven't seen since the Cold War.

Technology can be a major lubricant for needed change. The lockdowns are forcing the business and educational establishment to rethink the way they operate. The notion of workplace and work schedule is being transformed by remote access technology. The norms of higher education—the four-year college especially—are being redefined by remote learning in ways that may dent its unsustainable costs (and debt) imposed on students. The illogic and inequities of the American system of health care—provided mainly by employers—can no longer continue. Whether it's "Medicare for All" or a system closer to that of European and Asian democracies, there's a consensus for universal coverage. But in a country that already spends twice as much as the industrialized world per capita on health care, it will require aggressive use of technology to guarantee coverage in a way that does not bankrupt the country. Even as the West and China feuded in the wake of the COVID-19 outbreak—and the United States announced plans to pull out of the World Health Organization—countless researchers, scientists, and doctors were connecting across continents to study the virus and find a cure.

A fourth decade following the end of the Cold War is about to begin in an atmosphere of crisis and recrimination. Can we do better? Yes. Will we? I would argue we don't have a choice. Insanity is not destiny.

Acknowledgments

George Bernard Shaw wrote:

> *I want to be thoroughly used up when I die, for the harder I work the more I live. I rejoice in life for its own sake. Life is no "brief candle" for me. It is a sort of splendid torch which I have got hold of for the moment, and I want to make it burn as brightly as possible before handing it on to future generations.*

It is my passion to use my "splendid torch" to the fullest before passing it on to my grandchildren and their generation to do a far better job than my generation has done. They surely know what this country means to me, and how important it is to put country over party. Hence my motivation to write this book.

But I owe much to others who also pushed me to write it and played a major role in its creation. Two people stand out. Meg King has been my counselor and support system for over a decade: on my congressional staff, and then at the Wilson Center as my strategic advisor and the brilliant director of the Science and Technology Innovation Program. Thayer Scott was formerly chief speechwriter for Defense Secretary Robert Gates and is a thoughtful and deeply experienced craftsman. His research on my record and his enormous help in conceptualizing and writing this book are deeply appreciated.

Others who I spoke with about various chapters and who shared their extraordinary insights and experience are former CIA General Counsel Jeff Smith; Harvard Law School professor and former director of the Justice Department Office of Legal Counsel, Jack Goldsmith; former CIA and Defense Department Chief of Staff Jeremy Bash; Crowell & Moring's Cybersecurity Practice co-chair Evan Wolff; and Georgetown University's Ben Buchanan. They are valued friends and I am deeply grateful to them.

It was Tom Dunne of St. Martin's Press who persuaded me to write the policy book that many said would not attract readership. He and Stephen Power helped me get started, and their support was central to this effort. My agent, Matt Latimer, offered background and encouragement to bring the project to fruition. Matt is a *New York Times* bestselling author and was deputy director of speechwriting for President George W. Bush. His bipartisan literary and creative agency Javelin is impressive.

Personal thanks to Tim Bartlett of St. Martin's Press for editing the book and keeping us on a tight schedule.

And of course a shout-out to my colleagues at the Wilson Center, who demonstrate the value of scholarship and authorship every day. Special appreciation to Mary D'Amico, who helped me navigate a brutal calendar and still find time for writing.

Importantly, it is my family that provides the wind beneath my wings. My journalist daughter, Justine Harman, told me my initial title was boring and came up with the title I chose. She writes articles and produces podcasts and knows far better than I how readers and listeners respond. I am blessed to have her, three other amazing children, four stepchildren, and a large blended family to love and cherish.

Robert Frost wrote of "miles to go before I sleep." I surely hope this applies to me, and I can hold on to the "splendid torch" a while longer. So many mountains yet to climb—and so many hard problems yet to solve.

Jane Harman
Washington, D.C.

Bibliography

Acheson, Dean. *Present at the Creation: My Years at the State Department* (1968)

Aid, Matthew M. *The Secret Sentry: The Untold History of the National Security Agency* (2010)

Albright, Madeleine. *Madame Secretary* (2003)

Allen, Michael. *Blinking Red: Crisis and Compromise in American Intelligence After 9/11* (2016)

Alter, Jonathan. *The Center Holds: Obama and His Enemies* (2013)

Atkinson, Rick. *In the Company of Soldiers: A Chronicle of Combat in Iraq* (2004)

Baker, Peter. *Days of Fire: Bush and Cheney in the White House* (2013)

Bamford, James. *The Shadow Factory: The Ultra-Secret NSA from 9/11 to the Eavesdropping on America* (2009)

Berger, David H. (Gen. USMC). *Commandant's Planning Guidance: 38th Commandant of the Marine Corps* (2019)

Bickel, Alexander M. *The Least Dangerous Branch: The Supreme Court at the Bar of Politics* (1971)

Blackstock, Nelson. *Cointelpro: The FBI's Secret War on Political Freedom* (1988)

Bremer, L. Paul, III, and Maurice Sonnenberg. *Countering the Changing Threat of International Terrorism* (2000)

Brose, Christian. *The Kill Chain: Defending America in the Future of High-Tech Warfare* (2020)

Buchanan, Ben. *The Hacker and the State: Cyber Attacks and the New Normal of Geopolitics* (2020)

Burns, William J. *The Back Channel: A Memoir of American Diplomacy and the Case for Its Renewal* (2020)

Bush, George W. *National Security Strategy of the United States of America* (2002)

Chayes, Sarah. *Thieves of State: Why Corruption Threatens Global Security* (2015)

Cheney, Dick, et al. *Iran Contra Investigation Report, Section II: Minority Report* (1987)

Chertoff, Michael. *Homeland Security: Assessing the First Five Years* (2009)

Clapper, James R. *Facts and Fears: Hard Truths from a Life in Intelligence* (2018)

Clarke, Richard A. *Against All Enemies: Inside America's War on Terror* (2004)

Clarke, Richard A. *Cyber War: The Next Threat to National Security and What to Do About It* (2011)

Clarke, Richard A., and R. P. Eddy. *Warnings: Finding Cassandras to Stop Catastrophes* (2018)

Coll, Steve. *Ghost Wars: The Secret History of the CIA, Afghanistan, and Bin Laden from the Soviet Invasion to September 10, 2001* (2005)

Collins, Aukai. *My Jihad: The True Story of an American Mujahid's Amazing Journey from Usama Bin Laden's Training Camps to Counterterrorism with the FBI and CIA* (2011)

Continetti, Matt. *The K Street Gang: The Rise and Fall of the Republican Machine* (2006)

Daalder, Ivo H., and Michael E. O'Hanlon. *Winning Ugly: NATO's War to Save Kosovo* (2000)

Edgar, Timothy H. *Beyond Snowden: Privacy, Mass Surveillance, and the Struggle to Reform the NSA* (2017)

Feinstein, Dianne. *Senate Intelligence Committee Study on CIA Detention and Interrogation Program* (2014)

Ferraro, Geraldine A. *Framing a Life: A Family Memoir* (1998)

Fukuyama, Francis. *The End of History and the Last Man* (1992)

Garrett, Laurie. *The Coming Plague: Newly Emerging Diseases in a World out of Balance* (1994)

Gates, Robert M. *Duty: Memoirs of a Secretary at War* (2013)

Gellman, Barton. *Angler: The Cheney Vice Presidency* (2008)

Goldsmith, Jack. *The Terror Presidency: Law and Judgment Inside the Bush Administration* (2007)

Gourevitch, Philip, and Errol Morris. *The Ballad of Abu Ghraib* (2008)

Graham, Bob, Porter Goss, Nancy Pelosi, and Richard Shelby. *Joint Inquiry into Intelligence Community Activities Before and After the Terror Attacks of September 11, 2001* (2002)

Graham, Bob, and Jim Talent. *World at Risk: The Report of the Commission on the Prevention of WMD Proliferation and Terrorism* (2008)

Haass, Richard. *A World in Disarray: American Foreign Policy and the Crisis of the Old Order* (2017)

Haass, Richard N. *War of Necessity, War of Choice* (2010)

Hart, Gary, and Warren B. Rudman. *Roadmap for National Security: Imperative for Change* (2001)

Hayden, Michael V. *Playing to the Edge: American Intelligence in the Age of Terror* (2016)

Kagan, Robert. *The World America Made* (2012)

Kean, Thomas. *Final Report of the National Commission on Terrorist Attacks upon the United States* (2004)

King, Angus, and Michael Gallagher. *Report of the Cyberspace Solarium Commission* (2020)

Kissinger, Henry. *World Order* (2014)

Klaidman, Daniel. *Kill or Capture: The War on Terror and the Soul of the Obama Presidency* (2012)

Krepinevich, Andrew F. *Seven Deadly Scenarios: A Military Futurist Explores War in the Twenty-First Century* (2009)

Locker, James R., III. *Victory on the Potomac. The Goldwater-Nichols Act Unifies the Pentagon* (2004)

Mann, Thomas E., and Norman J. Ornstein. *Broken Branch: How Congress Is Failing America and How to Get It Back on Track* (2006)

Mayer, Jane. *The Dark Side: The Inside Story of How the War on Terror Turned into a War on American Ideals* (2009)

Mazzetti, Mark. *The Way of the Knife: The CIA, a Secret Army, and a War at the Ends of the Earth* (2013)

Miller, Judith, Stephen Engelberg, and William Broad. *Germs: Biological Weapons and America's Secret War* (2002)

Packer, George. *Our Man: Richard Holbrooke and the End of the American Century* (2019)

Panetta, Leon. *Worthy Fights: A Memoir of Leadership in War and Peace* (2014)

Pelosi, Nancy. *Know Your Power* (2008)

Powell, Colin. *My American Journey* (1995)

Power, Samantha. *"A Problem from Hell": America in the Age of Genocide* (2002)

Priest, Dana. *The Mission: Waging War and Keeping Peace with America's Military* (2003)

Ridge, Tom. *The Test of Our Times: America Under Siege . . . And How We Can Be Safe Again* (2009)

Risen, James. *State of War: The Secret History of the CIA and the Bush Administration* (2006)

Rizzo, John. *Company Man: Thirty Years of Controversy and Crisis at the CIA* (2014)

Roberts, Jerry. *Dianne Feinstein: Never Let Them See You Cry* (1994)

Rodriguez, Jose A., Jr. *Hard Measures: How Aggressive CIA Actions After 9/11 Saved American Lives* (2012)

Rumsfeld, Donald H. *Commission to Assess the Ballistic Missile Threat to the United States* (1999)

Savage, Charlie. *Power Wars: The Relentless Rise of Presidential Authority and Secrecy* (2015)

Sensenbrenner, James F., Jr., and John Conyers Jr. *The Administration's Use of FISA Authorities* (2013)

Silberman, Laurence H., and Charles S. Robb. *Report of the Commission on the Intelligence Capabilities of the United States Regarding Weapons of Mass Destruction* (2005)

Suskind, Ron. *The One Percent Doctrine: Deep Inside America's Pursuit of Its Enemies Since 9/11* (2006)

Taguba, Antonio. *Article 15-6 Investigation of the 800th Military Police Brigade* (2004)

Warrick, Joby. *Black Flags: The Rise of ISIS* (2015)

Weiner, Timothy. *Legacy of Ashes: The History of the CIA* (2007)

Wilson, Joe. *The Politics of Truth* (2004)

Wilson, Valerie Plame. *Fair Game* (2010)

Wine-Banks, Jill. *The Watergate Girl: My Fight for Truth and Justice Against a Criminal President* (2020)

Wright, Lawrence. *The Looming Tower: Al-Qaeda and the Road to 9/11* (2011)

Index